FOREWORD

Initially compiled in connection with an exhibit at the Library of Congress in the fall of 1968 observing the 30th anniversary of Atatürk's death and the 45th anniversary of the Turkish Republic, this bibliography has been expanded and its publication scheduled to coincide with the 50th anniversary of the establishment of the Turkish Republic. It responds to a wide need for a bibliography on contemporary Turkey, providing the librarian, the student, and the researcher in this country and elsewhere with a basic research instrument.

Included are books and periodical articles in western languages dealing with Kemal Atatürk (1881-1938), the founder and first president (1923-38) of the Republic of Turkey, and with Turkey under his leadership. Turkish-language materials are not included, because there are several extensive bibliographies on the subject in that language, e.g., Muzaffer Gökman's *Atatürk ve Devrimleri Tarihi Bibliyografyasi* (Istanbul, 1968), which also includes some western-language materials but fewer than this compilation.

The bibliography comprises 1,338 entries representing 560 books and 778 articles, located in 191 serial publications. Articles dealing with the period 1919-38, whether published during that time or later, are included. There are 57 entries authored by Turks as well as 16 issued from official Turkish sources. Only 106 entries are not located in the Library of Congress. The majority of items deal with the political life of Turkey during the Kemalist era; however, writings on history, geography, religion, economics, population, society, and education are also included. The entries are arranged alphabetically by author where known and otherwise by title. If the item is held by the Library of Congress, the call number is given.

The extensive subject index is based on key words selected from the titles to indicate the main subject of the book or article. Some subjects not appearing in the title have been listed to further help the reader locate the information he is seeking. To do this the content of the entries was searched, particularly for the names of the leading personalities that had a role in the Turkey of Atatürk. As an example, although the name of Rauf Orbay, a navy captain and a prime minister, does not appear in a title, he is the subject of an article, and therefore his name is indexed.

The periodicals searched for relevant articles are listed before the index. Mention should be made in this connection that only articles dealing with the period covered by the bibliography were searched for, whether these were published during that same period or later.

George N. Atiyeh
Head, Near East Section
Orientalia Division

National Union Catalog Symbols Used

ABS	Southern College, Birmingham
ABBS	[See: ABS]
CSt-H	Hoover Institution, Palo Alto, Calif.
ICU	University of Chicago
IU	University of Illinois, Urbana
MH	Harvard University, Cambridge, Mass.
NN	New York Public Library
NNC	Columbia University Library, New York, N. Y.
N. Y. P. L.	[See: NN]
OCU	University of Cincinnati Library
OU	Ohio State University, Columbus, Ohio
PPULC	Union Library Catalog, Philadelphia metropolitan area
ViU	University of Virginia, Charlottesville

CONTENTS

ATATÜRK
AND
TURKEY

A BIBLIOGRAPHY

1919–1938

Compiled by
ABRAHAM BODURGIL
Near East Section
Orientalia Division

LIBRARY OF CONGRESS   WASHINGTON   1974

Library of Congress Cataloging in Publication Data

Bodurgil, Abraham.
  Atatürk and Turkey:

  1. Turkey—History—1918-1960—Bibliography.
  2. Turkey—History—1960-   —Bibliography.
  3. Atatürk, Kamâl, Pres. Turkey, d. 1938-   —
Bibliography. I. United States. Library of Congress.
Near East Section. II. Title.
Z2850.B64   016.9561   73-18313
ISBN 0-8444-0112-9

**For sale by the Superintendent of Documents, U.S. Government Printing Office,
Washington, D.C. 20402—Price $1.20. Stock Number 3020—00011.**

BIBLIOGRAPHY

1

Abadan, Nermin. Mustafa Kemal Atatürk. *In* Hočevar, Rolf K. Politiker des 20. Jahrhunderts. München, Beck, 1970-71. p. 143-155.　　D412.6.H6

2

Abelous, Frederic. L'évolution de la Turquie dans ses rapports avec les étrangers. Toulouse, Impr. du Sud-Ouest, 1928. 297 p.　　JX4270.T9A3

3

The abolition of the Caliphate. Economist, v. 98, Mar. 8, 1924: 523-524.　　HG11.E2, v. 98

4

Aboltin, V. Natsionalnyĭ sostav poslelozanskoĭ Turtsii. Novyi vostok, no. 7, 1925: 115-129.
　　YUDIN JN18.N9, no. 7

5

Abrévaya, Juliette. La conférence de Montreux et le régime des Détroits. Paris, Les Editions Internationales, 1937. 172 p.　　DR741.B7A2

6

Adamov, E. A. Turtsiâ i velikie derzhavy. Mezhdunarodnaâ zhizń, no. 1, 1923: 9-26. D410.M4, no. 1

7

Adnan, Abdülhak (Adıvar). Ten years of republic in Turkey. Political quarterly, v. 6, Apr. 1935: 240-252.
　　JA8.P7, v. 6

8

Afetinan, A. The emancipation of the Turkish woman. Paris, Unesco, 1962. 63 p.　　HQ1707.A66

9

Afetinan, A. L'indépendance turque et le Traité de Lausanne. İstanbul, Devlet Basımevi, 1938, 307 p.
　　D462 1923 g

10

L'affaire d'Alexandrette. L'Asie française, v. 36, dèc. 1936: 314-327.　　JV1801.A85, v. 36

11

Ahlers, Johannes. Die Türkei von heute. Zeitschrift für politik, v. 18, Okt. 1929: 676-692. JA14.Z4, v. 18

12

Ahmed, Gulzar. Turkey; rebirth of a nation; a short history of the Turkish war of independence. Karachi, Ma'Aref, 1961. 206 p.　　DR589.A57

13

Akademiiâ nauk SSSR. Institut narodov Azii. Sovremennaiâ Turtsiâ. Moskva, Nauka, 1965.
335 p.　　DR593.A635

14

Aker, Zübeyir. Les produits du sol et du sous-sol, l'industrie et les transports dans l'économie nationale de la Turquie. Strasbourg, Librairie universitaire d'Alsace, 1936. 237 p.　　HC492.A63

15

Alâeddine, Haidar. A Angora auprés de Moustapha Kemal. Paris, Edition France Orient, 1921. 112 p.

16

Alekseev, E. Turtsiiâ, kak pynok sbyta tovarov sovetskoĭ promyshlennosti. Ekonomicheskii vestnik zakavkaz'iâ, v. 2, 15 fevr. 1925: 115-122.
　　HC337.T7A4, v. 2

17

Alekseev, V. M. Vneshniâiâ politika Turtsii. Moskva, Izd-vo, 1961. 94 p.　　DR477.A62

18

Alexinsky, Gregor. Bolshevism and the Turks. Quarterly review, v. 239, Jan. 1923: 183-197. AP4.Q2, v. 239

19

Allen, Henry E. The achievements of Ataturk. Yale review, v. 28, Mar. 1939: 542-557.   AP2.Y2, v. 28

20

Allen, Henry E. Factors in Turkey's cultural transformation. Open court, v. 46, May 1932: 331-342.
          AP2.O495, v. 46

21

Allen, Henry E. The outlook for Islam in Turkey. Moslem world, v. 24, Apr. 1934: 115-125.
          DS36.M7, v. 24

22

Allen, Henry E. The Turkish transformation; a study in social and religious development. Chicago, the University of Chicago press, 1935. 251 p. DR589.A6

23

Allen, W. E. Anatolian spring. Nineteenth century and after, v. 120, Oct. 1936: 452-459. AP4.N7, v. 120

24

Allen, W. E. Military aspects of the new Turkish railways. Army quarterly, v. 33, Oct. 1936: 28-38.
          U1.A85, v. 33

25

Allen, W. E. The Turkish mirror, 1928. Asiatic review, v. 24, Oct. 1928: 576-586.   DS1.A7, v. 24

26

Altnov, Ivan. Istoçno pitasiye i nova Turske. Sofia, 1929. 175 p.

27

Alvaro, Corrado. Viaggio in Turchia, con 36 illustrazioni. Milano, Edizioni Fratelli Treves, 1932. 225 p.   DR428.A7

28

Ambrosini, Gaspare. Regime degli Stretti. Roma, Istituto Nazionale Fascista di Cultura, 1937. 76 p.
          DR701.D2

29

America and the Turks. Missionary review of the world, v. 45, Nov. 1922: 853-855. BV2350.M7, v. 45

30

American committee for the independence of Armenia. The Lausanne treaty and Kemalist Turkey. New York, 1924. 79 p.   D462 1923 gr

31

American committee opposed to the Lausanne treaty. The Lausanne treaty, Turkey and Armenia. New York, 1936, 204 p.   D462 1926

32

American-Turkish commission. American-Turkish claims settlement. Under the agreement of December 24, 1923, and supplemental agreements between the United States and Turkey. Opinions and report prepared by Fred K. Nielsen. In accordance with the Act of March 22, 1935, 49 Stat. 67. Washington, U.S. Govt. print. off., 1937. 817 p.   JX238.T82

33

America's avoidance of duty in Turkey. World's work, v. 45, Dec. 1922: 235-240.   AP2.W8, v. 45

34

Amerika i Turtsiia. In Russia (1917-R.S.F.S.R.). Narodnoyi komissariat po inostrannym delam. Biulleten, no. 31, 15 sent. 1920: 31.   D411.R92, no. 31

35

Ampelas, Dēmētrios T. Hē kathodos tōn neōterōn myriōn. Athēnai, Deitepa Ekdosis, 1957. 318 p.

36

Anatoliia. In Russia (1917-R.S.F.S.R.). Narodnoyi komissariat po inostrannym delam. Biulleten, no. 33, 5 okt. 1920: 43-44.   D411.R92, no. 33

37

Anchieri, Ettore. Constantinopli e gli Stretti nella politica Russa ed Europea. Milano, Guiffrè, 1948. 268 p.   D465.A637

38

Anchieri, Ettore, Elio Migliorini, Nava Santi, and Rossi Ettore. La nuova Turchia. Roma, Edizioni Roma, 1939. 160 p.   NNC

39

Ancyranus. La Turchia Kemalista e il patto Italo-Turco. Gerarchia, v. 9, genn. 1929: 1-6.
          D410.G43, v. 9

40

Anderson, Paul. Impressions of modern Turkey. Contemporary review, v. 153, Jan. 1938: 26-34.
          AP4.C7, v. 153

41

Andréades, André. La Grèce et l'Asie Mineure. Revue de Genève, v. 3, sept. 1921: 409-418.

AP24.B44, v. 3

42

Andréades, André. Greece and Turkey. Contemporary review, v. 122, Aug. 1922: 167-173.

AP4.C7, v. 122

43

Andréades, André. Les puissances, la Grèce et la Turquie. Revue de Genève, v. 5, sept. 1922: 381-386.

AP24.B44, v. 5

44

Andrew, J. A. Turkey and the Middle East. *In* Laqueur, Walter Z. *ed.* The Middle East in transition; studies in contemporary history. Freeport, N. Y., . Books for Libraries Press, 1971. p. 187-195.

DS63.L36

45

Anglichane i Kemal. *In* Russia (1917-R.S.F.S.R.). Narodnoyi komissariat po inostrannym delam. Biulleten, no. 25, 25 iíul' 1920: 36.   D411.R92, no. 25

46

Angliĭskaia pechat'o Franko-Turetskom soglashanii. *In* Russia (1917-R.S.F.S.R.). Narodnoyi komissariat po inostrannym delam. Biulleten, no. 103, 28 noiabr 1921: 18-19.   D411.R92, no. 103

47

Angliĭskie plennye v Angore. *In* Russia (1917-R.S.F.S.R.). Narodnoyi komissariat po inostrannym delam. Biulleten, no. 86, 25 iíul' 1921: 32.

D411.R92, no. 86

48

Angliĭskie voĭska v Konstantinopole. *In* Russia (1917-R.S.F.S.R.). Narodnoyi komissariat po inostrannym delam. Biulleten, no. 74, 25 apr. 1921: 43.

D411.R92, no. 74

49

Angora i antanta. *In* Russia (1917-R.S.F.S.R.). Narodnoyi komissariat po inostrannym delam. Biulleten, no. 92, 20 sent. 1921: 87-88.   D411.R92, no. 92

50

Angora i mir. *In* Russia (1917-R.S.F.S.R.). Narodnoyi komissariat po inostrannym delam. Biulleten, no. 93, 25 sent. 1921: 45-46.   D411.R92, no. 93

51

Angora protiv Frantsii. *In* Russia (1917-R.S.F.S.R.). Narodnoyi komissariat po inostrannym delam. Biulleten, no. 86, 25 iíul' 1921: 32-33.

D411.R92, no. 86

52

Angorskie natsionalisty. *In* Russia (1917-R.S.F.S.R.). Narodnoyi komissariat po inostrannym delam. Biulleten, no. 80, 20 iíun 1921: 79. D411.R92, no. 80

53

Angorskiĭ protsess i vnutrenniaia politika Turtsii. Mezhdunarodnaia zhizn, no. 10, 1926: 71-73.

D410.M4, no. 10

54

Angorskoe ptaviteĺsvto i Serbiia. *In* Russia (1917-R.S.F.S.R.). Narodnoyi komissariat po inostrannym delam. Biulleten, no. 88, 10 avg. 1921: 42-43.

D411.R92, no. 88

55

Anikeev, P. SSSR i Turtsiia. Torgovlia Rosii s vostokom, no. 3-4, mart-maĭ 1925: 7-10.

Hc331.T58, no. 3-4

56

Anikeev, P. Torgovye oboroty SSR v Turtsii v 1923-1924 rodu. Torgovlia Rosii s vostokom, no. 3-4, mart-maĭ 1925: 5-8.   HC331.T58, no. 3-4

57

Antanta i blizhne-vostochnyĭ krizis. *In* Russia (1917-R.S.F.S.R.). Narodnoyi komissariat po inostrannym delam. Biulleten, no. 88, 10 avg. 1921: 35-38.

D411.R92, no. 88

58

Anthem, T. Russia and the Dardanelles. Contemporary review, v. 168, Oct. 1945: 222-226.

AP2.C698, v. 168

59

Antonoff, Nicolas. La Bulgarie et les Détroits. Politique étrangère, v. 17, nov. 1952: 361-378.

JX3.P6, v. 17

60

Aras, Tevfik R. 10 ans sur les traces de Lausanne. İstanbul, Akşam Matbaası, 1935. 278 p.

D462 1923 f

61

Armajani, Yahya The new Turkey. *In his* Middle

East: past and present. Englewood Cliffs, N. J. Prontice-Hall, 1970. p. 267-278.   DS62.A73

62
Armstrong, Harold C. Gray Wolf; the life of Kemal Ataturk. New York, Capricorn Books, 1961. 324 p.   DR592.K4A7

63
Armstrong, Harold C. Turkey, *In* Royal Central Asian Society. Journal, v. 15, part IV, 1928: 420-439.   DS1.R6, v.

64
Armstrong, Harold C. Turkey and Syria reborn; a record of two years of travel. London, John Lane, 1930. 270 p.   DR428.A8

65
Armstrong, Harold C. Turkey in travail; the birth of a new nation. London, John Lane, 1925. 280 p.   DR589.A8

66
Armstrong, Harold C. The Turkish women of today. North American review, v. 228, Aug. 1929: 199-205.   AP2.N27, v. 228

67
Arnold, Marguerite. Elegy for Atatürk. New republic, v. 98, May 3, 1939: 373-375.   AP2.N624, v. 98

68
Arsenev, N. Ocherki sovremennoĭ Turtsii. Novyi vostok, no. 2, 1922: 147-153.   YUDIN JN18.N9, no. 2

69
Arslan. Sovremonnaîă Turĭsiîă. Moskva, Krasnaîă Nov. 1923. 68 p.

70
Aschmann, Gottfried. Türkische wohlfahrt. Europäische revue, v. 12, Juni 1936: 507-509. AP30.E8, v. 12

71
Asopa, Sheel K. The foreign policy of modern Turkey, 1923-1968. Aligarh, Muslim University, 1971. 28 p.   DR477.A82

72
Astakhov, G. Ot sultanata k demokraticheskoi Turtsii; ocherki iz istorii Kemalizma. Moskva, Gos. Izd-Vo., 1926. 152 p.   DR592.D4A8

73
Ataturk. *In* Royal Central Asian Society. Journal, v. 26, Jan. 1939: 117-120.   DS.R6, v. 26
Signed: "A. T. W."

74
Atatürk, Kamâl, Pres. Turkey. d. 1938. Izbrannye rechi i vystupleniîă. Moskva, Progress, 1966. 438 p.   DR592.K4A26

75
Atatürk, Kamal, Pres. Turkey, d. 1938. A speech delivered by Ghazi Mustapha Kemal, President of the Turkish Republic, October 1927. Leipzig, K. F. Kochler, 1929. 724 p.   DR592.K4A323

76
Atay, Falih R. Atatürk. Europäische Revue, v. 12, Juni 1936: 433-442.   AP30.E8, v. 12

77
The attitude of Turkey. Economist, v. 96, Mar. 3, 1923: 486.   HG11.E2, v. 96

78
Aubrey, Herbert. New Turkey. Edinburgh review, v. 238, July 1923: 198-208.   AP4.E3, v. 238

79
"Augur". Europe, Turkey and Moscow. Fortnightly review, v. 125, Feb. 1926: 145-157.   AP4.F7, v. 125

80
Aurén, Sven A. Kemal slar naven ibordet. Stockholm, Albert Bonniers Förlag, 1934. 227 p.

81
L'avenir économique de la Turquie. L'Europe nouvelle, v. 11, juil. 1928: 1000-1005.   AP20.E88, v. 11

82
Ayling, Stanley E. Kemal Ataturk, 1881-1938. *In his* Portraits of power: an introduction to twentieth century history. London, Harrap, 1971. p. 33-49.   D412.6.A9

83
Bahrampour, Firouz. Turkey: political and social transformation. Brooklyn, Theo-Gaus' Sons, 1967. 100 p.   DR590.B28

84
Baird, A. Russia and Turkey; a study of Soviet inter-

ests in the Near East. Commonweal, v. 42, Sept. 14, 1945: 519-523.   AP2.C6897, v. 42

85
Bakeless, John. Actualities at Smyrna. Atlantic monthly, v. 133, Jan. 1924: 130-136.   AP2.A8, v. 133

86
Bakeless, John. Mustafa Kemal in the saddle. Atlantic monthly, v. 132, Dec. 1923: 825-832.
     AP2.A8, v. 132

87
Bakeless, John. The Turk comes to town. Atlantic monthly, v. 132, Nov. 1923: 687-696.   AP2.A8, v. 132

88
Baker, Robert L. Turkey and the Straits. Current history, v. 42, Sept. 1935: 666-667.   D410.C8, v. 42

89
Baker, Robert L. Turkey's five-year plan. Current history, v. 39, Mar. 1934: 761-762.   D410.C8, v. 39

90
Baker, Robert L. Turkey's nationalist creed. Current history, v. 42, June 1935: 441-443.   D410.C8, v. 42

91
Baker, Robert L. Turkey's new national assembly. Current history, v. 42, Apr. 1935: 106-107.
     D410.C8, v. 42

92
Baker, Robert L. Turkey's state-owned industries. Current history, v. 39, Feb. 1934: 632-633.
     D410.C8, v. 39

93
Baker, Robert L. The Turks build a nation. Current history, v. 39, Jan. 1934: 409-415.   D410.C8, v. 39

94
Baker, Robert L. Western ways for Turkey. Current history, v. 41, Jan. 1935: 505-506.   D410.C8, v. 41

95
Balas, Miloslav. Turecko včera a dnes. Praha, Orbis, 1940. 56 p.

96
Baldini, Antonio. Diagonale 1930, Parigi, Ankara; note di viaggio. Milano, A. Mondadori, 1943. 231 p.
     DC737.B3

97
Baldwin, Elbert F. The conquering Turk. Outlook, v. 134, Aug. 22, 1923: 619-621.   AP2.O8, v. 134

98
Baldwin, Elbert F. The former sick man. Outlook, v. 133, Feb. 14, 1923: 300-302.   AP2.O8, v. 133

99
Baldwin, Elbert F. The Turco-Bolshevist menace. Outlook, v. 132, Dec. 20, 1922: 698-699.
     AP2.O8, v. 132

100
Baldwin, Elbert F. The Turk who didn't go. Outlook, v. 132, Oct. 11, 1922: 232-233.   AP2.O8, v. 132

101
Baldwin, Elbert F. Will the Turk fight? Outlook, v. 142, Jan. 13, 1926: 52-54.   AP2.O8, v. 142

102
Bareilles, Bertrand. Le drame Oriental; d'Athènes à Angora. Paris, Editions Bossard, 1923. 272 p.   MH

103
Bartenev, O. Turt͡sii͡a; kratkii ekonomiko-politicheskii ocherk. Moskva, Izd. Tsk Mopr, 1927. 272 p.

104
Bassi, Ugo. L'Italia la nuova Turchia. Modena, E. Bassi e Nipoti, 1932. 56 p. NN   CSt-H

105
Başgil, Ali F. La question des Détroits. Paris, Paul Geuthner, 1928. 235 p.

106
Başgil, Ali F. La révolution militaire de 1960 en Turquie (ses origines); contribution à l'étude de l'histoire politique intérieure de la Turquie contemporaine. Genève, Perret-Gentil, 1963. 206 p.
     DR593.B3

107
Başgil, Ali Fuad, Sıddık Sami Onar *and* Cezmi Erçin. Turquie. Paris, Delagrave, 1939. 406 p.

108
Başgöz, M. İlhan, *and* Howard E. Wilson. Educational problems in Turkey. Bloomington, Indiana University, 1968. 268 p.   LA941.8.B3

109

Başman, Avni. Die Türkische sprachreform. Europäische revue, v. 12, Juni 1936: 512-519. AP30.E8, v. 12

110

Baumer, F. L. England, the Turk and the common corps of Christendom. American historical review, v. 50, Oct. 1944: 26-48. E171.A57, v. 50

111

Bayar, Turgut. La Türkiye iş bankasi (la Banque d'affaires de Turquie s. a.) et l'économie de la Turquie. Montreux, Imprimerie nouvelle C. Corbaz, s. a., 1939. 212 p. H3220.A6T812

112

Beauplan, Robert de. Resurgent Turkey and decadent Syria; Kemal and his Turkey. Living age, v. 348, May 1935: 222-227. AP2.L65, v. 348

113

Beckingham, C. F. Turkey: political institutions and foreign policy. University of Toronto quarterly, v. 29, Jan. 1960: 208-224. LH3.T6Q2, v. 29

114

Bednarska, Czesława. Turcja. Warszawa, Polskie Wydawnictwa Gospodarczo, 1951. 108 p. DR418.B4

115

Bekir-Sami vozvratilsiā v Parizh. In Russia (1917-R.S.F.S.R.). Narodnoyi komissariat po inostrannym delam. Biùlleten, no. 90, 30 avg. 1921: 57-58. D411.R92, no. 90

116

Belge, Burhan. Modern Turkey: with discussion. International affairs, v. 18, Nov. 1939: 745-762. JX1.I53, v. 18

117

Bello, C. G. Problème de guerre et de paix; notes et réflexions sur la Turquie. Paris, Boivin, 1921. 180 p. NN

118

Benoist-Mechin, Jacques G., *baron*. Le loup et le leopard; Mustapha Kémal ou la mort d'un empire. Paris, A. Michel, 1954. 438 p. DR592.K4B4

119

Bentwich, Norman D. Turkey after thirty years of the revolution. Quarterly review, v. 293, July 1955: 346-351. AP4.Q2, v. 293

120

Bentwich, Norman D. The Turkish constitutions, 1876-1942. Contemporary review, v. 162, Nov. 1942: 273-278. AP4.C7, v. 162

121

Bepard, Victor. La révolution Turque. Paris, Editeur Grasset, 1928. 189 p.

122

Bepard, Victor. La Turquie, l'Islam et les puissances. Paris, Editeur Grasset, 1930. 275 p.

123

Béraud, Henri. En Turquie: Mustapha Kemal, dictateur. *In his* Dictateurs d'aujourd'hui. Paris, Flammarion, 1933. p. 107-119. D412.6.B38

124

Berglund, Nils. Västra Turkiet i närbild. Stockholm, Generalstabens litografiska anstalt, 1966. 145 p. DR416.B45

125

Berkes, Niyazi. The development of secularism in Turkey. Montreal, McGill University Press, 1964. 537 p. DR557.B4

126

Berkes, T. Defending a dictator. Living age, v. 330, Sept. 4, 1926: 492-495. AP2.L65, v. 330

127

Berkol, Faruk N. L'évolution de l'entente Balkanique. Revue générale de droit internationale public, v. 46, juil.-août 1939: 472-496. JX3.R56, v. 46

128

Besnard, G. La Turquie pacifique. L'Asie française, v. 26, juin-juil. 1926: 222-226. JV1801.A85, v. 26

129

Bierstadt, Edward H. The great betrayal; a survey of the Near East problem. New York, R. M. McBride & Co., 1924. 345 p. D465.B5

130

Bigelow, Richard, *ed.* Turkey reborn. Scotch Plains, N. J., Flanders Hall, 1941. 96 p. DR589.B47

131

Bing, Edward J. Progress of women in new Turkey. Current history, v. 18, May 1923: 305-311. D410.C8, v. 18

132
Birge, John K. A guide to Turkish area study. Washington, Committee on Near Eastern Studies, American Council of Learned Societies, 1949. 240 p.
DR417.B5

133
Birge, John K. Secularism in Turkey and its meaning. International review of missions, v. 33, Oct. 1944: 426-432.	BV2351.I6, v. 33

134
Birge, John K. Turkey between two world wars. New York, Foreign Policy Ass'n., 1944. 208 p.	D410.F65

135
Birge, John K. Twelve years of the Turkish Republic. Missionary review of the world, v. 58, Mar. 1935: 118-120.	BV2350.M7, v. 58

136
Bisbee, Eleanor. How democratic is Turkey? Asia, v. 45, Feb. 1945: 86-89.	HF3119.A5, v. 45

137
Bisbee, Eleanor. The new Turks; pioneers of the Republic, 1920-1950. Philadelphia, University of Pennsylvania Press, 1951. 298 p.	DR590.B5

138
Bisbee, Eleanor. The people of Turkey. New York, The East and West Association, 1946. 43 p.
DR432.B5

139
Bisbee, Eleanor. Test of democracy in Turkey; structure of the Turkish government. Middle East journal, v. 4, April 1950: 170-182.	DS1.M5, v. 4

140
Bisbee, Eleanor. Turkey is pro-Turkish. Asia, v. 43, Mar. 1943: 139-143.	HF3119.A5, v. 43

141
Bischoff, Norbert. Ankara, eine Deutung des neuen Werdens in der Türkei. Wien, Leipzig, A. Holzhausens nachfolger, 1935. 226 p.	DR589.B5

142
Bischoff, Norbert. La Turquie dans le monde; l'Empire ottoman. La République turque. Paris, Payot, 1936. 247 p.	DR441.B5

143
Bismarck-Osten, Ferdinand. Strukturwandlungen und Nachkriegsprobleme der türkischen Volkswirtscaft Kiel, 1951. 104 p.	HC405.B5

144
Bjelavac, A. Reforme Mustafa Kemal Paše i njihov značaj u životu Muslimana. Život i rad, v. 12, 1933: 1291-1301.	AP56.Z5, v. 12

145
Black, Cyril E. The Turkish Straits and the great powers. Foreign policy reports, v. 23, Oct. 1, 1947: 174-182.	D410.F65, v. 23

146
Blacque, Josephine. The passing of the Greeks in Turkey. Current history, v. 18, Apr. 1923: 43-45.
D410.C8, v. 18

147
Blanco Villalta, Jorge G. Kemal Ataturk, el dictador democràtico, constructor de la nueva Turquia. Buenos Aires, Editorial Claridad, 1939. 516 p.
DR592.K4B5

148
Blanco Villata, Jorge G. El pueblo Turco. Buenos Aires, El Atenco, 1936. 244 p.	DR418.B6

149
Blijstra, Reinder. Reiziger in Turkije. Voor en voorbij de Bosporus. Amsterdam, De Arbeiderspers, 1966. 298 p.	DR429.B55

150
Böttiger, Theodor. Führer der völker. Berlin, Verlag Junge Generation, 1935. 204 p.

151
Bolender, Ernst. Die neue Türkische wirtschaft und wirtschaftspolitik. Berlin, P. Funk, 1931. 94 p.	MH
NN

152
Bomli, Pietar E. L'affaire de Mossoul. Amsterdam, H. J. Paris, 1929. 252 p.	DS51.M7B6

153
Bompard, Maurice. Impressions sur la Conférance de Lausanne. Boulogne-sur-Seine, Impr. d'Etudes sociales et politiques, 1923. 36 p. (Comité national d'études sociales et politiques. (Publications) fasc. no. 214)	D462 1923

154
Bonnafous, Max. Constantinople-Angora: tableaux de la Turquie nouvelle. La grande revue, v. 130, avril 1929: 224-235.   AP20.G7, v. 130

155
Boucher, José Le. D'Angora à Vilna. Paris, Èditions Prométhée, 1929. 252 p.   DR428.L4

156
Bourgoin, Marguerite. La Turquie d'Atatürk. Paris, E. Rey, 1936. 269 p.   DR428.B6

157
Bourgoin, Marguerite. Les dévoilées. Mercure de France, v. 259, l avril 1935: 50-68.   AP20.M5, v. 259

158
Boutierides, Elis P. Hē ekstratia para ton Sangariai. Athēnai, 1922. 63 p.

159
Bremoy, Guillaume de. La Conférance de Montreux et le nouveau régime des Détroits. Paris, Les Presses modernes, 1939. 230 p.   DR476.B7

160
Brikcius, M. Napric Kemalovym Tureckem. Praha, Nakladem Ceskoslovenske Graficke Unie, 1935. 119 p.

161
Brinton, Jasper Y. Turkey's new system of laws and courts. Current history, v. 25, Jan. 1927: 498-503.   D410.C8, v. 25

162
Bristol, Mark L. Papers, 1887-1939.   MS 60-20

163
Brock, Ray. Ghost on horseback; the incredible Atatürk. New York, Duell, Sloan & Pierce, 1954. 408 p.   DR592.K4B7

164
Broeder, Dirk L. Toerist in Turkije. Utrecht, Ons Huis, 1970. 168 p.   DR417.B77

165
Brosse, P. B. de la. L'évolution sociale et économique de la Turquie et le commerce français. L'Asie française, v. 35, déc. 1935: 318-322.   JV1801.A85, v. 35

166
Brown, Constantine. Chance and the cards in Near Eastern diplomacy. Asia, v. 23, Feb. 1923: 127-130, 149-150.   HF3119.A5, v. 23

167
Brown, Constantine. Tragicomic exit of the Osman dynasty. Asia, v. 24, June 1924: 449-453.   HF3119.A5, v. 24

168
Brown, F. Yeats. Turkey today and tomorrow. Spectator, v. 142, Feb. 2, 1929: 150-151.   AP4.S3, v. 142

169
Brown, Philip M. From Sèvres to Lausanne. American journal of international law, v. 18, Jan. 1924: 113-116.   JX1.A6, v. 18

170
Brown, Philip M. The Lausanne conference. American journal of international law, v. 17, Apr. 1923: 290-296.   JX1.A6, v. 17

171
Browne, Lawrence E. Religion in Turkey, today and tomorrow. Moslem world, v. 19, Jan. 1929: 14-24.   DS36.M7, v. 19

172
Brunton, Chisholm D. Passing of Islam in Turkey. English review, v. 50, May 1930: 592-599.   AP4.E523,v. 50

173
Bruzon, Paul. La déchéance du Sultan et la question du Khalifat. L'Europe nouvelle, v. 5, 25 nov. 1922: 1482-1484.   AP20.E88, v. 5

174
Bryant, Louise. A Turkish divorce. Nation, v. 121, Aug. 26, 1925: 231-232.   AP2.N2, v. 121

175
Bujac, Émile. Les campagnes de l'armée Hellénique, 1918-1922. Paris, Charles Lavauzelle, 1930. 348 p.   MH

176
Buonocore, Biagio. Constantinopoli. Napoli, Tipografia Portasalvo, 1927. 54 p.

177
Burhans, Barent. Recreational developments in Tur-

key. Recreation, v. 25, Nov. 1931: 428-430.
GV421.R5, v. 25

178
Burnouf, Denis. Turcorama. Paris, Hachette, 1967.
231 p. DR420.B86

179
Burr, Pamela. My Turkish adventure. New York,
Norton, 1951. 219 p. DR432.B8

180
Burroughs, Franklin. Robert College and Turkish
advancement. Moslem world, v. 54, Oct. 1964:
288-291. DS36.M7, v. 54

181
Burton, H. M. Development of modern Turkey. *In*
Royal Central Asian society. Journal, v. 29, Jan.
1942: 17-29. DS1.R6, v. 29

182
Burton, H. M. Modern Turkey. Geographical magazine, v. 13, May 1941: 1-17. G1.G343, v. 13

183
Butaev, N. Natsionalnaià revoliùtsiià na vostoke pro-
blemi Turtsii. Leningrad, Pribozh, 1925. 213 p.

184
Buzanski, Peter M. Admiral Mark L. Bristol and
Turkish-American relations, 1919-1922. PhD. dis-
sertation, University of California, 1960.

185
Cambó y Batlle, Francisco de Asis. Visions d'Orient.
Barcelona, Editorial Catalana, 1924. 165 p.
D463.C3

186
Can Islam be reformed? The Turkish answer. Moslem
world, v. 16, July 1926: 238-252. DS36.M7, v. 16

187
Candida, Luigi. La Turchia. Roma, Cremonese, 1942.
111 p. PPULC

188
Carter, W. L. In Anatolia. Life and letters today, v. 32,
Feb. 1942: 99-105. AP4.L416, v. 32

189
Carter. W. L. New educational system of Turkey. Life

and letters today, v. 25, Apr. 1940: 10-18.
AP4.L416, v. 25

190
Castle, Wilfrid T. Grand Turk; an historical outline
of life and events, of culture and politics, of trade
and travel during the last years of the Ottoman
Empire and the first years of the Turkish Republic.
New York, Hutchinson, 1943. 170 p. DR557.C36

191
Cataluccio, Francesco. La questione degli Stretti;
studio storico-diplomatico. Milano, Istituto per gli
Studi di Politica Internazionale, 1936. 32 p. MH

192
Caucig, Franz. Türkei. 4. ergänzte und erweiterte
Aufl. Bonn, K. Schroeder, 1964. 416 p. DR416.C3

193
Caucig, Franz. Um die Zukunft des Kemalismus in
der Türkei. Aussenpolitik, v. 19, Okt. 1968:
627-634. D839.A885, v. 19

194
Cebe, Jaroslav. Anglie a Turecko. Otázka Mossulska.
Praha, Orbis, 1928. 89 p.

195
Celâl, Ömer (Sarç). Die wirtschafliche strukturder
Türkei. Europäische revue, v. 12, Juni 1936:
463-474. AP30.E8, v. 12

196
Chambrun, Charles, *compte de*. Atatürk et la Turquie
nouvelle. Paris, Fernand Sorlot, 1939. 47 p.
DR592.K4C45

197
Chambrun, Charles, *compte de*. De Stamboul à
Ankara; ma première entrevue avec Ghazi Mustapha Kemal. Revue des deux mondes, v. 47, 1 oct.
1938: 772-796. AP20.R3, v. 47

198
Chandler, Douglas. The transformation of Turkey.
National geographic magazine, v. 75, Jan. 1939:
1-50. G1.N27, v. 75

199
Changing ideas in Turkey. Sphere, v. 102, Aug. 22,
1925: 244. AP4.S73, v. 102

200
Chatterton-Hill, Georges. The rebuilding of Istanbul. Contemporary review, v. 149, Mar. 1936: 351-356.   AP4.C7, v. 149

201
Les chemins de fer turcs. L'Asie française, v. 29, avr. 1929: 120-124.   JV1801.A85, v. 29

202
Chesnai, P. G. L'Arménie, Angora et Moscou. Action nationale, v. 18, mars 1922: 185-188.   AP20.A3, v. 18

203
Chester, Arthur T. Angora and the Turks. Current history, v. 17, Feb. 1923: 758-764.   D410.C8, v. 17

204
Chester, Arthur T. History's verdict on new Turkey's rise to power. Current history, v. 19, Oct. 1923: 79-86.   D410.C8, v. 19

205
Chester, Colby M. Some political aspects of American trade in Turkey. Boston City Club bulletin, v. 18, Nov. 1923: 27-30.   HS275.B7C615, v. 18

206
Chester, Colby M. Turkey reinterpreted. Current history, v. 16, Sept. 1922: 939-947.   D410.C8, v. 16

207
Chirgwin, A. M. A new Turkey. Nineteenth century and after, v. 99, Mar. 1926: 356-363.   AP4.N7, v. 99

208
Chirol, *Sir* Valentine. The downfall of the Khilafate. Foreign affairs, v. 2, June 15, 1924: 571-582.   D1.F6, v. 2

209
Chrisochos, Athanasios. To Hellēnikon hypikon kata tēn Mikrasiatikēn ekstratian; 1919-1922. Athēnai, 1934. 384 p.

210
Clerget, Marcel. La Turquie, passé et présent. Paris, A. Colin, 1938. 207 p.   DR417.C55

211
Cleveland, C. O. Kemal the victorious. Commonweal, v. 29, Nov. 25, 1938: 118-120.   AP2.C6897, v. 29

212
Cohen, Albert. Le kemalisme; préface du president Edouard Herriot. Paris, F. Alcan, 1937. 298 p.
                      DR589.C57

213
Cohn, Edwin J. Turkish economic, social, and political change; the development of a more prosperous and open society. New York, Praeger, 1970. 196 p.
                      HC405.C57

214
Cole, Seymour. England should know Turkey; a short story of the renovation of Turkey. Istanbul, Hachette, 1940. 162 p.

215
Colliard, Claude A. La Convention de Montreux; nouvelle solution du probleme des Détroits. Revue de droit international, v. 10, juil./sept. 1936: 121-152.   JX3.R35, v. 10

216
Collins, J. Walter. Kemal the victorious. Asia, v. 34, Mar. 1934: 138-139.   HF3119.A5, v. 34

217
Collins, J. Walter. Modern Turkey. *In* Royal Central Asian Society. Journal, v. 19, Apr. 1932: 234-253.
                      DS1.R6, v. 19

218
Collins, J. Walter. The situation in Turkey. Contemporary review, v. 138, Oct. 1930: 452-458.
                      AP4.C7, v. 138

219
Collins, J. Walter. Ten years of Kemalism. Contemporary review, v. 144, Aug. 1933: 182-191.
                      AP4.C7, v. 144

220
Collins, J. Walter. The Turco-Greek rapprochement. Contemporary review, v. 139, Feb. 1931: 203-208.
                      AP4.C7, v. 139

221
Collins, J. Walter. The Turkish census and what it means. Contemporary review, v. 133, Feb. 1928: 194-200.   AP4.C7, v. 133

222
Colrat, Raymond. Lausanne et les vieillards; autour

d'une conférence. Paris, Armand Collin, 1923.
224 p.   MH

223
Colrat, Raymond. Turkey today. Living age, v. 333,
July 1927: 129-134.   AP2.L65, v. 333

224
Combescure, Ferdinand. L'abolition du Khalifat et
l'Afrique française. Revue mondiale, v. 158,
15 mars 1924: 164-166.   AP20.R25, v. 158

225
Conference on Political Modernization in Japan and
Turkey, Gould House, 1962. Political moderniza-
tion in Japan and Turkey; edited by Robert E.
Ward and Dankwart Rustow. Princeton, N. J.,
Princeton University Press, 1964. 502 p. JQ1622.C6

226
Conker, Orhan. Les chemins de fer en Turquie et la
politique ferroviaire turque. Paris, Librairie du
Recueil Sirey, 1935. 192 p.   HE3225.C6

227
Conker, Orhan. Redressement économique et industrialisation de la nouvelle Turquie. Paris, Librairie
du Recueil Sirey, 1937. 345 p.   HC405.C6

228
Contenson, Ludovic de. La question Turque vue
d'Asie. Correspondant, v. 298, 10 jan. 1925: 90-102.
                                    AP20.C8, v. 298

229
A convalescent sick man. Youth's companion, v. 97,
Aug. 9, 1923: 476-477.   AP201.Y8, v. 97

230
Cornwell, J. H. A journey in Anatolia. Geographical
journal, v. 64, Sept. 1924: 213-222.   G7.R91, v. 64

231
Council on Turkish-American relations. New Orient,
v. 2, Apr.-June 1925: 79-96; v. 3, July 1926: 89-96.
                                    DS501.N6, v. 2, 3

232
Council on Turkish-American Relations. The treaty
with Turkey, why it should be ratified. New York,
Council on Turkish-American Relations, 1926.
164 p.   DR479.U5C6

233
Courson, Guy de. L'oeuvre d'Ataturk. Revue de
Paris, v. 45, 1 déc. 1938: 606-630.   AP20.R27, v. 45

234
Couzinos, Efthimios N. Twenty-three years in Asia
Minor (1899-1922). New York, Vantage Press, 1969.
175 p.   DR583.C68

235
Cox, Col. Clifton F. Turkish army's role in nation
building. Military review, v. 47, April 1967: 68-74.
                                    Z6723.U35, v. 47

236
Crabbe, Geoffrey. Turkey: a record of industrial and
commercial progress in the last quarter of a century. In Royal Central Asian Society. Journal, v.
31, Jan. 1944: 48-63.   DS1.R6, v. 31

237
Crabitès, Pierre. Is Turkey a Mohammedan country?
Moslem world, v. 20, Apr. 1930: 125-137.
                                    DS36.M7, v. 20

238
Crabitès, Pierre. Mustafa Kemal Ghazi and his hat.
Moslem world, v. 18, Oct. 1928: 388-391.
                                    DS36.M7, v. 18

239
Crain, Maurice. Kemal Ataturk. In his Rulers of the
world. New York, Thomas Y. Crowell, 1940. p. 201-
234   D412.7.C7

240
Cramer, A. G. Turkey in search of protectors: an excursion into the history of a strategic area. Current
history, n. s. v. 13, Oct.-Nov. 1947: 210-216, 280-287.
                                    D410.C8, v. 13

241
Creasy, Sir Edward S. Turkey. New York, P. F. Collier,
1939. 614 p.   D20.H62

242
Crouzet, Pierre. Pourquoi Ismet Pacha a quitté
Lausanne. Revue hebdomadaire, v. 3, 3 mars 1923:
90-99.   AP20.R55, v. 3

243
Crow, W. L. Kemal's Turkey. Dalhousie review, v. 15,
July 1935: 199-211.   AP5.D3, v. 15

244
Daniel, Robert L. The Armenian question and American-Turkish relations, 1914-1927. Journal of American history, v. 46, Sept. 1959: 252-275.
E171.J87, v. 46

245
Daniel, Robert L. The United States and the Turkish republic before World War II: the cultural dimension. Middle East journal, v. 21, Winter 1967: 52-63.
DS1.M5, v. 21

246
Danilov, Vladimir I. Srednie sloi v politicheskoi zhizni sovremennoi Turtsii v period podgotovki i provedeniià gosudarstvennogo perevorota 27 maia 1960 g. Moskva, Nauka, 1968. 149 p.   DR593.D35

247
Danne, René de. En passant par Stambul. Mercure de France, v. 247, 1 nov. 1933: 601-613. AP20.M5, v. 247

248
Dantsig, Boris M. Perspektivy torgovykh otnosheniĭ SSSR s Turtsieĭ. Novyi vostok, no. 10-11, 1925: 152-160.   YUDIN JN18.N9, no. 10-11

249
Dantsig, Boris M. Turetskaià Respublika. Moskva, Znanie, 1956. 38 p.   JA34.V83

250
Dantsig, Boris M. Turtsiià. Moskva, Voei. izd-vo, 1949. 308 p.   DR418.D3

251
Dardanelles; war laps at both ends of Turkey's trouble spot. Life, v. 13, Nov. 16, 1942: 98-102.
AP2.L547, v. 13

252
Darling, Marjorie. Journey to Ankara. New York, Macmillan, 1954. Unpaged.   PZ7.D249Jo

253
Davidson, Basil. Britain helps Turkey to arm. Sphere, v. 154, July 16, 1938: 90-91, 114. AP4.S73, v. 154

254
Davis, Fanny E. Getting to know Turkey. New York, Coward-McCann, 1957. 64 p.   DR428.D4

255
Davison, Roderic H. Middle East nationalism: Lausanne 30 years after. Middle East journal, v. 7, Summer 1953: 324-348.   DS1.M5, v. 7

256
Davison, Roderic H. Turkey. Englewood Cliffs, N. J., Prentice-Hall, 1968. 181 p.   DR441.D24

257
Davison, Roderic H. Turkish diplomacy from Mudros to Lausanne. Princeton, Princeton University Press, 1953. 176 p.

258
Davison, W. S. New lights in Turkey. Christian century, v. 49, Nov. 16, 1932: 1407-1410.
BR1.C45, v. 49

259
Dejardin, André. Turquie 1955; que reste-t-il de la révolution Kémalienne? La revue nouvelle, v. 21, 15 mai 1955: 528-536.   AP22.R72, v. 21

260
Deklaratsiià Mustafy-Kemalià-pashi. In Russia (1917-R.S.F.S.R.). Narodnoyi komissariat po inostrannym delam. Biulleten, no. 100, 7 noiàbr 1921: 36-37.
D411.R92, no. 100

261
Delegatsiià Kemal'-pashi. In Russia (1917-R.S.F.S.R.). Narodnoyi komissariat po inostrannym delam. Biulleten, no. 67, 5 mart 1921: 42-43.
D411.R92, no. 67

262
Demirel, Esat. La Banque Agricole de Turquie. Lausanne, G. Risoldet fils, 1935. 80 p.

263
Dennis, Alfred L. The United States and the new Turkey. North American review, v. 217, June 1923: 721-731.   AP2.N7, v. 217

264
Deny, Jean. Souvenirs du Gâzi Moustafa Kemâl Pacha. Paris, Geuthner, 1927. 463 p.   D566.A813

265
Deny, Jean and René Marchand. Petit manuel de la Turquie nouvelle. Paris, J. Haumont, 1934. 318 p.
DR589.D4

266
Denny, Ludwell. The Turk comes back. Nation, v. 115, Nov. 29, 1922: 575-577.   AP2.N2, v. 115

267

D'escola, Marguerite. La vie à Angora et la nouvelle Turquie. Revue de France, v. 11, 1 mai 1931: 51-57.
AP20.R2663, v. 11

268

Development in Turkey: a survey of 25 years' progress. Asiatic review, n. s. v. 45, April 1949: 617-621.
DS1.A7, v. 45

269

Devereux, Robert. Turkish economic doctrine and organization, old and new. Social science, v. 37, April 1962: 99-107.
H1.S55, v. 37

270

Dewey, John. Impressions of Soviet Russia and the revolutionary world: Mexico, China, Turkey. New York, New republic, 1929. 270 p. Turkey, 1924: The Turkish tragedy; Angora the new; Secularizing a theocracy. p. 195-234.
DK267.D4

271

Diamandapoulos, H. Le réveil de la Turquie. Paris, Albin Michel, 1926. 173 p.

272

Dictator caps 16-year labors with unpublicized war and political pact. Newsweek, v. 9, June 26, 1937: 8-10.
AP2.N6772, v. 9

273

Diéval, *Mme.* Renée *and* S. Reshad, *bey.* Kemal pacha Ata-Türk; sa vie et son oeuvre. Oran, Heintz frères, 1939. 101 p.
DR592.K4D45

274

Digoy, Charles. L'incendie de Smyrne. Revue de Paris, v. 31, 1 avril 1924: 645-667.   AP20.R27, v. 31

275

Djafer, Tayyar (Kankat). Étude philosophique et analyse psychologique sur les origines de I — l'ultrapopularisme de philosophie moderne de Kemal Atatürk; II—la civilisation turque actuelle; III—l'émancipation de la femme turque. Paris, Librairie Orientaliste Paul Geuthner, 1935. 112 p.

276

Djonker, Mahmud C. Le Bosphore et les Dardanelles; les conventions des Dètroits de Lausanne (1923) et Montreux (1936). Lausanne, 1938. 164 p
JX1393.S8D56

277

Dodd, C. H. Politics and government in Turkey. Berkeley, University of California Press, 1969. 335 p.
JN9715.D6

278

Dollerup, Preben. Det moderna Turkiet. Stockholm, Rabén & Sjögren, 1962. 32 p.   DR592.A1D6

279

Donovan, John M. The government of Turkey. Washington, 1925. 62 p.   Law: 52-51067

280

Dourmoussis, Evdokimos. La vérité sur un drame historique; la catastrophe de Smyrne, Septembre 1922. Paris, Coffin, 1928. 160 p.   DS51.I9D6

281

Dousmanēs, Biktōr. Hē esōterikē opsis tēs Mikrasiatikēs emplokēs. Athēnai, 1928.   DF845.D68

282

Downing Street and the Dardanelles. Economist, v. 95, Sept. 23, 1922: 495-496.   HG11.E2, v. 95

283

Dragos, Gheorghe. Kemal Ataturk. Cluj, Omulopera, 1935. 48 p.

284

Dragoslav, Mihailoviç. Priveda savremene Turske. Beograd, Beletra, 1937. 180 p.

285

Drucker, Peter F. Turkey and the balance of power. Atlantic monthly, v. 167, Apr. 1941: 462-469.
AP2.A8, v. 167

286

Du Véou, Paul. Le désastre d'Alexandrette, 1934-1938. Paris, Edition Baudiniere, 1938. 175 p.

287

Du Véou, Paul. La passion de la Cilicie, 1919-1922. Paris, Librairie orientaliste P. Geuthner, 1954. 448 p.   DS51.C5D8

288

Duda, Herbert W. Vom Kalifat zur Republik; die Türkei im 19. und 20. Jahrhundert. Wien, Verlag für Jugend und Volk, 1948. 183 p.   DR577.D8

289
Duggan, Stephen P. Turkish gains out of Western discords. *In* American Academy of Political and Social Science. Annals, v. 108, July 1923: 148-152.
H1.A4, v. 108

290
Duhamel, Georges. La Turquie nouvelle, puissance d'occident. Paris, Mercure de France, 1954. 125 p.
DR590.D8

291
Dukagjin-Zadeh, Basri. La paix turque et les Balkans. Revue de Genève, v. 7, août 1923: 254-258.
AP24.B44, v. 7

292
Dukagjin-Zadeh, Basri. La Turquie en republique. Revue de Geneve, v. 8, avril 1924: 505-512.
AP24.B44, v. 8

293
Dunn, Robert. Kemal, the key to India and Egypt. World's work, v. 44, May 1922: 57-67. AP2.W8, v. 44

294
Duteil, Honri-Jean. Loin dans la Turquie. Paris, La Table Ronde, 1958. 252 p.   DR429.D8

295
Earle, Edward M. The new constitution of Turkey. Political science quarterly, v. 40, Mar. 1925: 73-100.
H1.P8, v. 40

296
Earle, Edward M. Our holier than thou policy. Forum, v. 72, Dec. 1924: 740-745.   AP2.F8, v. 72

297
Earle, Edward M. Ratify the Turkish treaty. Nation, v. 118, Jan. 23, 1924: 86-88.   AP2.N2, v. 118

298
Earle, Edward M. Turkey, the Great Powers, and the Baghdad Railway; a study in imperialism. New York, Russell, 1966. 364 p.   D463.E2

299
Eaton, Richard. Mustapha Kemal à Smyrne. Revue hebdomadaire, v. 10, 14 oct. 1922: 209-214.
AP20.R55, v. 10

300
Economics and politics in Turkey. Economist, v. 111, Nov. 29, 1930: 992.   HG11.E2, v. 111

301
Edberg, Rolf. "den sjuke mannen" som blev frisk. Tiden, v. 30, dec. 1938: 595-601.   HX8.T5, v. 30

302
Edib, Halide (Adıvar). Rising star of Mustapha Kemal. Asia, v. 28, July 1928: 570-576.
HF3119.A5, v. 28

303
Edib, Halide (Adıvar). Turkey faces west; a Turkish view of recent changes and their origin. New Haven, Yale university press, 1930. 273 p.
DR441.A37

304
Edib, Halide (Adıvar). The Turkish ordeal. New York, The Century co., 1928. 407 p.   DR592.A4A35

305
Edib, Halide (Adıvar). Woman's part in Turkey's progress. Open court, v. 46, May 1932: 343-360.
AP2.O495, v. 46

306
Education under Mustafa Kemal. School and society, v. 46, Dec. 4, 1937: 727-728.   L11.S36, v. 46

307
Edwards, George W. Constantinople, Istamboul. Philadelphia, The Penn Publishing Co., 1930. 312 p.
DR722.E4

308
Edwards, L. F. The Near East: a survey; brief review of social and economic conditions; Turkey. Geographical magazine, v. 23, Nov. 1950: 289-295.
G1.G343, v. 23

309
Efendieva, N. Z. Borba turetskogo naroda protiv frantsuzskikh okkupantov na iuge Anatolii, 1919-1921 gg. Baku, Izd-Vo Akademii Nauk Azerbaidzhanskoi SSR, 1966. 158 p.   DR589.E33

310
Eger, Hans. Die gegenwärtigen völkerrechtlichen Beziehungen der Türkei. Greifswald, Buchdruckerei Hans Adler, 1924. 81 p.

311
Ekrem, Mustafa. Le contrôle de l'execution du budget en Turquie. Paris, Domat-Montchrestien, 1937. 178 p.   HJ1288.E4

312
Ekrem, Selma. Turkey, old and new. New York, C. Scribner's Sons, 1947. 186 p.   DR432.E33

313
Ekrem, Selma. Unveiled; the autobiography of a Turkish girl. New York, I. Washburn, 1930. 320 p.   DR432.E35

314
Ellis, E. D. The evolution of Turkish political institutions. Current history, n.s. v. 13, Dec. 1947: 347-351; v. 14, Feb. 1948: 95-99.   D410.C8, v. 13 & 14

315
Ellis, William T. Jennings of Smyrna. Scribner's, v. 84, Aug. 1928: 230-235.   AP2.S4, v. 84

316
Ellis, William T. Will the anchor hold? The Turkish government at Angora. American review of reviews, v. 68, Sept. 1923: 159-161.   AP2.R4, v. 68

317
Ellison, Grace M. An Englishwoman in Angora; with 34 illustrations reproduced from the author's own sketches and photographs. London, Hutchinson, 1923. 344 p.   DR589.E4

318
Ellison, Grace M. Turkey today. London, Hutchinson, 1928. 288 p.   DR432.E45

319
Elston, Roy. How Atatürk rode to power. Sphere, v. 155, Nov. 19, 1938: 290.   AP4.S73, v. 155

320
Emerson, Mabel E. The outlook for the women of Turkey today. Moslem world, v. 15, July 1925: 269-273.   DS36.M7, v. 15

321
Engelmann, Gerhard. Bosphorus und Dardanellen. Geographischer anzeiger, v. 43, Juli/Aug. 1942: 258-271.   G1.G39, v. 43

322
Enukidze, D. Desiât' let Turetskoĭ Respubliki. Mirovoe khoziaĭstvo i mirovaia politika, no. 10, okt. 1933: 86-93.   HC10.K536, no. 10

323
Eren, Nuri. Turkey today and tomorrow; an experiment in westernization. New York, Praeger, 1963. 276 p.   DR593.E68

324
Erkin, Feridun C. Les relations turco-soviétiques et la question des détroits. Ankara, 1968. 540 p.   JX1393.S8E69

325
Essen, R. Bakom Asiens portar. Stockholm, Albert Bonniers Förlag, 1931. 220 p.

326
Eubank, Earle E. Social reconstruction in Turkey. Journal of applied sociology, v. 9, July 1925: 450-456.   HM1.J6, v. 9

327
European statecraft again fails in Turkey. World's work, v. 45, Nov. 1922: 12-14.   AP2.W8, v. 45

328
Evans, Frederic. The Anglo-Turkish alliance. Empire review, v. 70, July 1939: 29-31.   DA10.C5, v. 70

329
Evans, Laurence. United States policy and the partition of Turkey, 1914-1924. Baltimore, Johns Hopkins Press, 1965. 437 p.   E183.8.T8E9

330
L'évolution économique de la Turquie. L'Asie française, v. 37, déc. 1937: 300-303.   JV1801.A85, v. 37

Signed: "F. T."

331
Evrenol, Hilmi M. Revolutionary Turkey. Istanbul, Hachette, 1936. 145 p.   DR418.E8

332
Eylan, Claude. Nouvelle Turquie. Revue des deux mondes, v. 38, 15 mars 1937: 421-440.   AP20.R3, v. 38

333
Fairchild, J. A. Turkey: Gibraltar of the Middle East; general progress since 1923. United States Naval

Institute proceedings, v. 80, Feb. 1954: 168-175.

V1.U8, v. 80

334
Faraut, Léon. France et Turquie. Action nationale, v. 21, nov. 1923: 314-315.   AP20.A3, v. 21

335
Farrère, Claude. Turquie ressuscitée. Paris, Editions des Cahiers Libres, 1930. 154 p.

336
Faugères, G. Peytavi de. La resurrection de la Turquie et la France. Revue mondiale, v. 151, 15 nov. 1922: 152-161.   AP20.R25, v. 151

337
Fekete, Imre. A "Törökök atyja", Musztafa Kemál. Élet ès tudomany kalendariuma, v. 23, 1968: 2144-2147.   Q9.E45, v. 23

338
Fenwick, Charles G. The new status of the Dardanelles. American journal of international law, v. 30, Oct. 1936: 701-706.   JX1.A6, v. 30

339
Feyzioğlu, Turhan. Les partis politiques en Turquie; du parti unique à la démocratie. Revue française de science politique, v. 4, Jan.-Mar. 1954: 131-155.   JA11.R6, v. 4

340
Filipenko, D. M. Druzi i vorohy revoliutsiinoi Turechchyny (1918-1922). Kiev, Naukova dumka, 1968. 210 p.   DR589.F55

341
The Financial times, London. Republic of Turkey supplement. London, 1937. 48 p.   HC405.F5

342
Fischer, A. J. Turkish foreign policy. Free Europe, v. 4, Oct. 31, 1941: 249-250.   D731.F7, v. 4

343
Fisher, Sydney N., Edwin J. Cohn, *and* Walter F. Weiker. Turkey. *In* Collier's encyclopedia, with bibliography and index. New York, Crowell-Collier Educational Corp., 1970, v. 22. p. 527-551. AE5.C683

344
Forbes, Rosita (Torr). Conflict; Angora to Afghanistan. New York, Frederick A. Stokes, 1931. 333 p.   DS49.5.F55

345
Forbes, Rosita T. Two presidents of Turkey: Ataturk and Ismet Ineunu. *In her* These men I knew. New York, E. P. Dutton, 1940. p. 157-174.   D412.6.F6

346
Foreign policy association. *New York.* The Turco-American treaty of amity and commerce signed at Lausanne, August 6, 1923; a report of the F. P. A. Committee on the Lausanne treaty, presented May, 1924, to the Executive Committee of the Foreign Policy Association. New York, 1924. 31 p. (F. P. A. Pamphlet no. 27. Series of 1923-1924).   JX1428.T9F7

347
Fox, Annie E. Islam and modern education. Moslem world, v. 23, Jan. 1933: 29-37.   DS36.M7, v. 23

348
France. Ministère des Affaires Étrangères. Bulletin périodique de la presse Grècque, 1920-1936. Paris, Imprimerie Nationale.

349
France. Ministère des Affaires Étrangères. Bulletin périodique de la presse Turque, 1920-1936. Paris, Imprimerie Nationale.

350
Franco, Gad. Développements constitutionnels en Turquie. Paris, Rousseau et cie., 1925. 160 p.

JN9715.F7

351
Frey, Frederick W. The Turkish political elite. Cambridge, M. I. T. Press, 1965. 483 p.   DR590.F7

352
Frey, Ulrich. Die Karte der neuen Türkei. Petermanns geographische Mitteilungen, v. 81, Sept.-Okt. 1935: 363-364.   G1.P43, v. 81

353
Frödin, John. La morphologie de la Turquie sud-est. Geografiska annaler, v. 19, 1937: 1-29. G25.G4, v. 19

354
Frödin, John. Quelques traits de la végétation et de l'habitat pastoral de la Turquie du Nord. Geografiska annaler, v. 14, 1932: 209-243.   G25.G4, v. 14

355
Froembgen, Hanns. Kamal Atatürk, soldat und führer. Stuttgart, Franckh, 1935. 222 p.
DR592.K4F7

356
Froidevaux, Henri. Ce que la paix de Lausanne a fait de la Turquie et des intérêts français en Turquie. L'Asie française, v. 23, août-sept. 1923: 262-266. JV1801.A85, v. 23

357
Froidevaux, Henri. L'effondrement des Grecs et ses conséquences. L'Asie française, v. 22, sept.-oct. 1922: 325-328. JV1801.A85, v. 22

358
Froidevaux, Henri. Les négotiations de Lausanne et leur suspension. L'Asie française, v. 23, jan.-fèv. 1923:8-10. JV1801.A85, v. 23

359
Froidevaux, Henri. Les responsibilités du president de la république de Turquie. L'Asie française, v. 23, nov. 1923: 382-383. JV1801.A85, v. 23

360
Froidevaux, Henri. La séparation des pouvoirs politiques en Turquie. L'Asie française, v. 22, nov. 1922: 379-380. JV1801.A85, v. 22

361
Les funérailles émouvantes du fondateur de la Turquie nouvelle. L'Illustration, v. 201, 10 déc. 1938: 491-494. AP20.I3, v. 201

362
Furniss, Edgar S. A new state faces a difficult world; the position of Turkey today. New Haven, Yale literary magazine, 1940. 83 p. DR589.F8

363
Gaillard, Gaston. The Turks and Europe. London, Thomas Murky & Co., 1921. 408 p. D651.T9G3

364
Gajek, Józef. Kemal Pasza, dyktator Turecki. Warszawa, Universum, 1933. 64 p.

365
Galib, Rachid. Smyrna during the Greek occupation. Current history, v. 18, May 1923: 318-319.
D410.C8, v. 18

366
Garle, H. E. Some modern aspects of the capitulations. In Royal Central Asian Society. Journal, v. 19, July 1932: 412-433. DS1.R6, v. 19

367
Gaspari, G. Ankara e la Turchia Kemalista. Vie del mondo, v. 5, nov. 1937: 1197-1221. G1.V53, v. 5

368
Gateau, Jean J. Moustapha Kemal. L'Europe nouvelle, v. 5, 7 oct. 1922: 1258. AP20.E88, v. 5

369
Gates, Caleb F. The making of the Turkish republic. Current history, v. 34, Apr. 1931: 89-93.
D410.C8, v. 34

370
Gates, Caleb F. New Turkey under Mustapha Kemal. Current history, v. 34, June 1931: 390-394.
D410.C8, v. 34

371
Gates, Caleb F. Not to me only. Princeton, Princeton University Press, 1940. 340 p. LF5236.G3A3

372
Gates, Caleb F. The regeneration of Turkey. Current history, v. 32, June 1930: 519-528. D410.C8, v. 32

373
Gates, Caleb F. The Turkish transformation. Moslem world, v. 26, Apr. 1936: 186-192. DS36.M7, v. 26

374
Gault, Henri. La Turquie de Henri Gault et Christian Millau. Paris, Julliard, 1968. 132 p. DR416.G3

375
Gavin, Catherine I. The house of war. New York, Morrow, 1970. 350 p. PZ3.G24.Hq3

376
Gazi Mustafa Kemâl Atatürk; founder of the Turkish Republic. Ankara, Turkish Ministry of Press, Broadcasting and Tourism, 1961. 301 p.
DR592.K4G39

377
Gen. Pellé o Franko-Turetskom soglashenii. In Russia (1917-R.S.F.S.R.). Narodnoyi komissariat inostrannym dclam. Biulleten, no. 106, 19 dek. 1921: 32. D411.R92, no. 106

378
Gentizon, Paul. Constantinople versus Angora. Living age, v. 320, Mar. 29, 1924: 600-604.
AP2.L65, v. 320

379
Gentizon, Paul. Mustapha Kemal, ou L'Orient en marche. Paris, Éditions Bossard, 1929. 350 p.
DR589.G35

380
Georges-Gaulis, Berthe. Angora. Orient et occident, v. 3, oct. 1922: 154-206.   DS1.045, v. 3

381
Georges-Gaulis, Berthe. Angora, Constantinople, Londres; Moustafa Kémal et la politique Anglaise en Orient. Paris, A. Colin, 1922. 257 p.   DR589.G4

382
Georges-Gaulis, Berthe. Ce qui sont les gens d'Angora. L'Opinion, v. 15, 18 fév. 1922: 174-175.
AP20.06, v. 15

383
Georges-Gaulis, Berthe. Constantinople entre Paris et Londres. Orient et occident, v. 3, nov. 1922: 336-384.   DS1.045, v. 3

384
Georges-Gaulis, Berthe. Conversation avec Mustapha Kémal Pacha. L'Opinion, v. 15, 4 mars 1922: 230-231.   AP20.06, v. 15

385
Georges-Gaulis, Berthe. En Anatolie; la bataille et la retraite d'août et septembre 1922. Orient et occident, v. 4, 15 jan. 1923: 23-46.   DS1.045, v. 4

386
Georges-Gaulis, Berthe. Le gouvernement d'Angora. Revue hebdomadaire, v. 10, 21 oct. 1922: 343-358.
AP20.R55, v. 10

387
Georges-Gaulis, Berthe. In the land of Kemal Pasha. Living age, v. 312, Mar. 11, 1922: 573-576.
AP2.L65, v. 312

388
Georges-Gaulis, Berthe. Moustafa Kémal Pacha. Orient et occident, v. 2, août 1922: 446-476.
DS1.045, v. 2

389
Georges-Gaulis, Berthe. Le nationalisme Turc. Paris, Librairie Plon, 1921. 148 p.

390
Georges-Gaulis, Berthe. La nouvelle Turquie. Paris, A. Colin, 1924. 282 p.   DR589.G45

391
Georges-Gaulis, Berthe. Les origines intelectuelles du nationalisme Turc. Orient et occident, v. 2, juin 1922: 171-193.   DS1.045, v. 2

392
Georges-Gaulis, Berthe. La question Turque; une page d'histoire Turque et d'erreurs Européenes 1919-1931. Paris, Berger-Levrault, 1931. 373 p   ViU
IU
NN

393
Gérando, Félix de. La Turquie nouvelle. Paris, Arthème Fayard, 1927. 137 p.

394
Gerard, J. W. The Lausanne treaty; should the United States ratify it? New York, Foreign Policy Ass'n. pamphlet No. 26, 1924. 31 p.   D839.3.F6, No. 26

395
Giannini, Amedeo. La costituzione Turca. Oriente moderno, v. 5, febbr. 15, 1925: 65-80.   D461.07, v. 5

396
Giannini, Amedeo. Kemal Atatürk. *In his* Uomini politici del mio tempo; profili. Milano, Istituto per gli Studi di Politica Internazionale, 1942. p. 193-201.
D412.6.G5

397
Giannini, Amedeo. Il regime degli Stretti dopo gli atti di Montreux. Oriente moderno, v. 18, ott. 1938: 527-536.   D461.07, v. 18

398
Gignoux, C. J. La conférence de Lausanne et les intérêts économiques de la France en Turquie. L'Action nationale, v. 19, déc. 1922: 294-297.
AP20.A3, v. 19

399
Gillespie, Julian E. Economic policy of the new Turkish republic. *In* U.S. Bureau of Foreign and

Domestic Commerce. Commerce reports, no. 52, Dec. 29, 1924: 745-747.   HC1.R21, no. 52

400
Gillespie, Julian E. Slow reconstruction work continues in Turkey. *In* U.S. Bureau of Foreign and Domestic Commerce. Commerce reports, no. 43, Oct. 22, 1928: 205-207.   HC1.R21, no. 43

401
Gilman, William. Turkey offers her own ism. South Atlantic quarterly, v. 38, Oct. 1939: 377-391.
          AP2.S75, v. 38

402
Gilman, William. Turkey with western dressing: almost all recovered, a once "sick" nation is about ready to play Europe at its own game. Current history, v. 49, Nov. 1938: 37-39.   D410.C8, v. 49

403
Giritli, İsmet. Fifty years of Turkish political development, 1919-1969. İstanbul, Fakülteler Matbaası, 1969. 228 p.   JN9715.G57

404
Glasgow, George. Turkey and the Straits. Contemporary review, v. 149, June 1936: 740-742.
          AP4.C7, v. 149

405
Glasneck, Johannes. Kemal Atatürk und die moderne Türkei. Berlin, Deutscher Verlag der Wissenschaften, 1971. 331 p.   DR592.K4G57

406
Godden, G. M. Kemal, the man and the movement. Fortnightly review, v. 118, Nov. 1922: 718-723.
          AP4.F7, v. 118

407
Godes, Mikhail S. Chto takoe Kemalistskiĭ puť i vozmozhen li on v Kitae? Leningrad, Izd-vo Priboĭ. 1928. 109 p.

408
Gökman, Muzaffer. Bibliography of the history of Atatürk and his reforms. Istanbul, Millî Eğitim Basımevi, 1968. 697 p.   DR592.K4A854

409
Goldfarb, A. Mustafa Kemal pasha. Mezhdunarodnaĭa zhizn, no. 12, 1922: 14-17.   D410.M4, no. 12

410
Gontaut-Biron, *Compte* Roger de, *and* L. Le Révérend. D'Angora à Lausanne; les étapes d'une déchéance. Paris, Plon-Nourrit, 1924. 226 p.
          D469.F8G6

411
Gordlevskii, Vladimir A. Izbrannie sochinniĭa, v. 3. Moskva, Izd. vost. lit., 1962. 588 p.

412
Gordon, Leland J. American relations with Turkey, 1830-1930; an economic interpretation. Philadelphia, University of Pennsylvania Press, 1932. 402 p.   HF3114.G6

413
Gordon, Leland J. Turkish-American treaty relations. American political science review, v. 22, Aug. 1928: 711-721.   JA1.A6, v. 22

414
Graeco-Turkish war of 1920. Balkan review, v. 4, Sept. 1920: 81-93.   D461.B3, v. 4

415
Graves, Philip P. The Anglo-Turkish agreement. Listener, v. 21, May 18, 1939: 1027-1028.
          AP4.L4165, v. 21

416
Graves, Philip P. Briton and Turk. London, Hutchinson, 1941. 260 p.   DR471.G7

417
Graves, Philip P. Question of Alexandretta. Nineteenth century and after, v. 124, Aug. 1938: 158-168.   AP4.N7, v. 124

418
Graves, Philip P. The question of the Straits. London, Allen & Unwin, 1929. 278 p.   D372.G7

419
Graves, Philip P. The question of the Straits. *In* Royal Central Asian Society. Journal, v. 20, Jan. 1933: 7-26.   DS1.R6, v. 20

420
Graves, Philip P. Turkey's key position. Listener, v. 21, Nov. 2, 1939: 853-858.   AP4.L4165, v. 21

421

The great battle for Angora. Current history, v. 15, Oct. 1921: 143-145. D410.C8, v. 15

422

Gt. Brit. Naval Intelligence Division. Turkey. Oxford, University Press, 1942-43. 2 v. DR417.G7

423

Greece and Turkey. Near east, v. 24, Dec. 13. 1923: 610-611. D461.G8, v. 24

424

The Greek débacle. Saturday review, v. 134, Sept. 9, 1922: 373-374. AP4.S3, v. 134

425

Greenwald, Norman D. Kemal Ataturk: modernizer of Turkey. *In his* Portraits of power. Cambridge, Mass., Berkshire Pub. Co., 1961. p. 51-60. D412.6.G7

426

Greenwall, H. J. Turkey with the fez off. Sphere, v. 139, Nov. 10, 1934: 222-223. AP4.S73, v. 139

427

Greko-Turetskaia voĭna. *In* Russia (1917-R.S.F.S.R.). Narodnoyi komissariat po inostrannym delam. Biulleten, no. 74, 25 apr. 1921: 42-43.
D411.R92, no. 74

428

Gretsiia i Smirna. Mezhdunarodnaia zhizn, no. 1, 1922: 35-36. D410.M4, no. 1

429

Gretsiia i voĭna v Maloĭ Azii. *In* Russia (1917-R.S.F.S.R.) Narodnoyi komissariat po inostrannym delam. Biulleten no. 82, 5 iiul 1921: 31.
D411.R92, no. 82

430

Gretsiia, Turtsiia i antanta. Mezhdunarodnaia zhizń, no. 10, 1922: 43. D410.M4, no. 10

431

Grew, Joseph C. Turbulent era; a diplomatic record of forty years, 1904-1945. Boston, Houghton Mifflin, 1952. 1560 p. E748.G835A3

432

Grĭns, Aleksandrs. Mustafa Kemals, jaunas Turcijas nodibinatajs. Riga, Izdevis A. Gulbis, 1935. 188 p.

433

Gueron, E. Turkey believed ready to disarm. Christian century, v. 50, Aug. 2, 1933: 993. BR1.C45, v. 50

434

Gueron, E. Turkey mourns Kemal's death. Christian century, v. 56, Jan. 4, 1939: 31-32. BRI.C45, v. 56

435

Guest, L. Haden. Turkey as it is. Spectator, v. 134, June 13, 1925: 962-963. AP4.S3, v. 134

436

Gurko-Kriazhin, V. A. Istoriia revolutsii ve Turtsii. Moskva, Mir. 1923. 196 p.

437

Gurko-Kriazhin, V. A. Politicheskie gruppirovki v Turtsii. Novyi vostok, no. 3, 1923: 35-66.
YUDIN JN18.N9, no. 3

438

Gurko-Kriazhin, V. A. Voznik-novenie natsionalno-osvoboditelnogo dvizheniia v Turtsii. Novyi vostok, no. 23-24, 1928: 268-275.
YUDIN JN18.N9, no. 23-24

439

Haegstad, Tove M. Tyrkiet. København, Carit Andersen, 1967. 231 p. DR429.H3

440

Hagimihali, Platon. La vie économique de la Turquie et ses relations commerciales avec la Grèce. Les Balkans, v. 2, juil. 1932: 463-468. DR1.B35, v. 2

441

Hall, Josef W. Mustapha Kemal. *In his* Eminent Asians. New York, D. Appleton, 1929. p. 249-338.
DS32.H3

442

Hall, Melvin. Flight over the Turkish republic. Travel, v. 67, Oct. 1936: 6-12. G149.T73, v. 67

443

Hall, Melvin. Men around the Gazi. Asia, v. 36, Sept. 1936: 607-610. HF3119.A5, v. 36

444

Hall, Melvin. Turkey's fear of Italy. Asia, v. 35, Nov. 1935: 707. HF3119.A5, v. 35

445
Hamburger Kreditbank A. G. Türkei; wirtschaftlicher Lagebericht. Hamburg, 1951. 63 p. HC405.H3

446
Hamdi, Abdullah F. The burning of Smyrna. Current history, v. 17, Nov. 1922: 317. D410.C8, v. 17

447
Hanson, A. H. Turkey today; economic and political progress. Political quarterly, v. 26, Oct.-Dec. 1955: 323-335. JAS.P72, v. 26

448
Hanusets, Oleksandr I. Derzhavnyĭ ustriĭ Turechchyny v period respubliky. Kiev, Vid-vo Akademii nauk Ukr. PSR, 1961. 94 p. JN9711.H2

449
Harbord, James G. Mustapha Kemal Pasha and his party. World's work, v. 40, June 1920: 176-193. AP2.W8, v. 40

450
Harington, *Sir* Charles. Mudania and Chanak, 1922. Quarterly review, v. 275, Oct. 1940: 277-290. AP4.Q2, v. 275

451
Harington, *Sir* Charles. Tim Harington looks back. London, J. Murry, 1940. 288 p. DA69.3.H33A3

452
Harper, W. A. The Gazi of Turkey. Journal of religion, v. 13, Jan. 1933: 1-17. BR1.J65, v. 13

453
Harris, Elizabeth. How Mustapha Kemal formed his army. Current history, v. 17, Nov. 1922: 295-299. D410.C8, v. 17

454
Harris, George S. The origins of communism in Turkey. Stanford, Hoover Institution, 1967. 215 p. HX357.H36

455
Harris, George S. The role of the military in Turkish politics—Part I. Middle East journal, v. 19, Winter 1965: 54-66. DS1.M5, v. 19

456
Harrison, Marguerite E. Angora, birthplace of the new Turkey. Travel, v. 43, Oct. 1924: 6-12, 36. G149.T75, v. 43

457
Hartmann, Hans W. Die auswärtige Politik der Türkei, 1923-1940. Zürich, Gebr. Leemann, 1941. 64 p. DR476.H3

458
Hartmann, Hans W. L'évolution politique et sociale de la Turquie Kemaliste. Les Balkans, v. 7, août-oct. 1935: 185-203. DR1.B35, v. 7

459
Hartmann, Hans W. Die neue Türkei; 1923-1933. Zürich, Neue Zürcher Zeitung, 1933. 48 p.

460
Hartmann, Hans W. Les relations gréco-turques du Traité de Lausanne au Pacte d'Ankara. Les Balkans, v. 11, oct.-déc. 1939: 333-350. DR1.B35, v. 11

461
Hartmann, Richard. Im neuen Anatolien; Reise-eindrücke. Leipzig, J. C. Hinriehs, 1928. 148 p. DS49.3.H27

462
Has the Turk become speakable? Outlook, v. 142, Apr. 7, 1926: 516. AP2.08, v. 142

463
Hasan, Beni. Kemal Pasha at home; the new master of Turkey. Mentor, v. 15, May 1927: 20-22. AP2.M417, v. 15

464
Heathcote, Dudley. Mustapha Kemal and the new Turkey. Fortnightly review, v. 127, Jan 1927: 74-84. AP4.F7, v. 127

465
Heathcote, Dudley. The new Turkey. Contemporary review, v. 125, May 1924: 576-583. AP4.C7, v. 125

466
Hecker, G. Der völkerrechtliche Wohnsitzbegriff: Untersuchungen in Anknupfung an den griechisch-turkischen Streit uber den Bevolkerungsaustausch. Berlin, Walther Rothschild, 1931. 87 p. JX4241.H4

467
Hell, Vera. Istanbul und die vordere Türkei. Tübingen, Hopfer, 1966. 270 p. DR416.H412

468
Heller, Deane F. Hero of modern Turkey: Atatürk. New York, J. Messner, 1972. 190 p.   DR592.K4H43

469
Hellssen, Henry. The Turkish soldier and the Sakaria march. Living age, v. 319, Oct. 20, 1923: 123-126.   AP2.L65, v. 319

470
Hemingway, Ernest. The wild years. New York, Dell Pub. Co., 1962. 288 p.   PS3515.E37A16

471
Henze, Paul B., *and* Dankwart A. Rustow. Turkey. *In* Hammond, Thomas T. *comp.* Soviet foreign relations and world communism; a selected, annotated bibliography of 7000 books in 30 languages. Princeton, N. J., Princeton University Press, 1965. p. 863-875.   Z2517.R4H3

472
Herbert, *Hon.* Aubrey N. Ben Kendim, a record of eastern travel. New York, G. P. Putnam's sons, 1925. 380 p.   DR428.H4

473
Herriot, Édouard. Orient. Paris, Hachette, 1934. 418 p.   D443.H44

474
Herrmann, Gerhard. Die Dardanellen. Leipzig, W. Goldmann, 1936. 97 p.   DR701.D2H47

475
Hershlag, Zvi Y. Turkey: achievements and failures in the policy of economic development during the inter-war period 1919-39. Kyklos, v. 7, 1954: 323-350.   H1.A15, v. 7

476
Hershlag, Zvi Y. Turkey; the challenge of growth. Leiden, E. J. Brill, 1968. 406 p.   HC405.H47

477
Heydt, Uriel. Islam in modern Turkey. *In* Royal Central Asian Society. Journal, v. 34, July-Oct. 1947: 299-308.   DS1.R6, v. 34

478
Heyersberg, Fritz A. Maschinenverwendung im Wirtschaftsleben der Türkei. Berlin, E. Ebering, 1934. 136 p.   HC405.H48

479
Hills, Dennis C. My travels in Turkey. London, Allen & Unwin, 1964. 252 p.   DR429.H5

480
Hindbeck, Hanna. Der wind schlägt um am Bosporus; tagebuch eines einfachen Türken. Berlin, Atlantis-verlag, 1935. 207 p.   DR432.H52

481
Hinterhoff, Eugène. The advance on Angora and the battle for Warsaw: a parallel in military history. Asiatic review, v. 30, Oct. 1934: 652-680.   DS1.A7, v. 30

482
Horton, George. The blight of Asia. Indianapolis, Bobbs Merrill, 1926. 292 p.   DS51.S7H6

483
Houille, René. La politique monétaire de la Turquie depuis 1929. Paris, Sirey, 1937. 148 p.   HG1164.H68

484
Housepian, Marjorie. The Smyrna affair. New York, Harcourt Brace Jovanovich, 1971. 269 p.   DS51.I9H68

485
Hovannisian, Richard G. The republic of Armenia; vol. I, the first year, 1918-1919. Berkeley, University of California Press, 1971. 547 p.   DS195.5.H56

486
How Turkey failed Russia at Lausanne. Literary digest, v. 78, Sept. 15, 1923: 22-23.   AP2.L58, v. 78

487
Howard, Harry N. The partition of Turkey; a diplomatic history, 1913-1923. Norman, University of Oklahoma Press, 1931. 486 p.   DR577.H6

488
Howard, Harry N. The problem of the Turkish Straits. Washington, U. S. Govt. print. off., 1947. 68 p.   DR741.B7H6

489
Howard, Harry N. The reduction of Turkey from an empire to a national state. Open court, v. 46, May 1932: 291-305.   AP2.0495, v. 46

490
Howard, Harry N. The Straits after the Montreux Conference. Foreign affairs, v. 15, Oct. 1936: 199-202.   D410.F6, v. 15

491
Howard Harry N. Turkey goes industrial. Current history, v. 45, Oct. 1936: 99-104.   D410.C8, v. 45

492
Howard, Harry N. Turkish foreign policy. Asia, v. 38, Jan. 1938: 29-31.   HF3119.A5, v. 38

493
Howard, Harry N. The United States and Turkey: American policy in the Straits question, 1914-1963. Balkan studies, v. 4, 1963: 225-250.
                                        DR1.B32, v. 4

494
Huddleston, Sisley. Mustapha Kemal: the Napoleon of the new Turkey. *In his* Those Europeans; studies of foreign faces. New York, Putnam's, 1924. p. 253-266.   D412.6.H8

495
Hudson, Geoffrey F. Guardian of the Straits. Listener, v. 21, Nov. 1939: 1060-1063.   AP4.L4165, v. 21

496
Hudson, Geoffrey F. Turkey, Greece and the eastern Mediterranean. Oxford, The Clarendon press, 1939. 32 p. (Oxford pamphlets on world affairs, no. 9).   D463.H8

497
Hudson, Manley O. Admission of Turkey to membership in the League of Nations. American journal of international law, v. 26, Oct. 1932: 813-814.
                                        JX1.A7, v. 26

498
Hüber, Reinhard. Die Türkei, ein weg nach Europa. Berlin, Volk und reich Verlag, 1943. 103 p.
                                        DR418.H8

499
Hüseyin Ragıp. Le mouvement national turc et Moustapha Kemal Pacha. Paris, Stock Editeur, 1922. 125 p.

500
Hughes, Charles E. The Near East, Turkey. American journal of international law, v. 18, Apr. 1924: 237-243.   JX1.A6, v. 18

501
Hurewitz, Jacob C., *ed.* Diplomacy in the Near and Middle East; a documentary record: 1914-1956, v. 2, 1956. 427 p.   DS42.H78

502
Hurewitz, Jacob C. Documents of Near East diplomatic history. New York, Near and Middle East Studies, School of International Affairs, Columbia University, 1951. 332 p.   DS42.H8

503
Hurewitz, Jacob C. Middle East politics: the military dimension. New York, published for the Council on Foreign Relations, by Praeger, 1969. 553 p.   DS62.8.H8

504
Hurgronje, Snouck. Islam and Turkish nationalism. Foreign affairs, v. 3, Sept. 15, 1924: 61-77.
                                        D40.F6, v. 3

505
Hussein, Kadria, *Princess of Egypt.* Lettres d'Angora, la Sainte; Avril-Juin 1921. Rome, Imp. Editrice Italia, 1921. 267 p.

506
Hyde, Walter W. The transformation of Turkey. World unity, v. 11, Oct. 1932: 20-29.
                                        AP2.W755, v. 11

507
Imbrie, Robert W. Crossing Asia Minor, the country of the new Turkish Republic. National geographic magazine, v. 46, Oct. 1924: 445-472.   GI.N27, v. 46

508
Industrial development of Turkey. European economic and political survey, v. 3, Sept. 15, 1927: 12-16.   HC10.E8, v. 3

509
Influence of modern Turkish literature upon Turkish westernization. Moslem world, v. 21, Oct. 1931: 401-407.   DS36.M7, v. 21

510
Irandust. Neskol'ko slov o Kemalizme. Revoliutsionnyĭ vostok, no. 8, 1930: 53-71.   DS1.N353, no. 8

511
Irandust. Sushchnost́ Kemalizma. Za partiiu, no. 2,
1927: 62-69.   JN6598.K4Z2, no. 2

512
Ireland, Philip W. Turkish foreign policy after
Munich. Political quarterly, v. 10, Apr. 1939:
185-201.   JA8.P72, v. 10

513
İşbay, Sami. Das Finanzwesen der Türkischen Republik. Europäische revue, v. 12, Juni 1936: 475-482.
                                        AP30.E8, v. 12

514
Ĭuasunski, M. S. Ocherk gosudarstvennogo ustro-
ĭstva Turetskoi Respubliki. Moskva, 1925. 69 p.

515
Ĭuoldzu. Borba vokrug alfavita; pismo iz Konstanti-
nopoliâ. Novyi vostok, no. 15, 1926: 293-301.
                              JUDIN JN18.N9, no. 15

516
Ĭust, Konstantin. Kemalizm. Krasnaiâ nov́, v. 6, sent
1926: 165-177.   AP50.K73, v. 6

517
Ĭust, Konstantin. Zhenskoe dvizhenie v Turtsii; pis’-
mo iz Angory. Krasnaiâ nov’, no. 8, 1928: 194-196.
                                       AP50.K73, no. 8

518
Ivanov, L. Turtsiiâ i rezhim prolivov. Mirovoe kho-
ziaistvo i mirovaia politika, no. 6, 1936: 79-87.
                                       HC10.K536, no. 6

519
İyriboz, Nihat. Neuordnung der Landwirtschaft.
Europäische Revue, v. 12, Juni 1936: 482-490.
                                        AP30.E8, v. 12

520
Jackh, Ernest. The rising crescent; Turkey yesterday,
today, and tomorrow. New York, Farrar & Rine-
hart, 1944. 278 p.   DR577.J3

521
Jackson, Barbara W. Turkey. New York, Oxford University Press, 1942. 121 p.   DR418.J3

522
Jahn, Hans E. Türkei mit Stadtführer Istanbul, Ankara und Reiserouten. Buchenhain vor München,

Verlag Volk und Heimat, 1963. 184 p.   DR416.J3

523
Jäschke, Gotthard, Ankara, die Hauptstadt der
Türkischen Republik. Europäische Revue, v. 12,
Juni 1936: 457-463.   AP30.E8, v. 12

524
Jäschke, Gotthard. Der Islam in der neuen Türkei;
eine rechtsgeschichtliche Untersuchung. Leiden,
E. J. Brill, 1951. 174 p.   DS36.W4

525
Jäschke, Gotthard. Mustafa Kémal et la proclamation de la Republique en Turquie. Orient, v. 7,
no. 27, 1963: 29-44.   DS1.044, v. 7

526
Jäschke, Gotthard. Le role du communisme dans
les relations Russo-Turques de 1919 a 1922. Orient,
v. 7, no. 26, 1963: 31-44.   DS1.044, v. 7

527
Jäschke, Gotthard. Die Türkei in den jahren 1935-
1941, Geschichtskalender mit Personen und Sach-
register. Leipzig, O. Harrassowitz, 1943. 194 p.
                                          DR589.J28
528
Jäschke, Gotthard, and Erich Pritsch. Die Türkei
seit dem Weltkriege. Berlin, Deutsche Gesellschaft
für Islamkunde, 1929-1931. 168 p.   DR589.J3

529
Jalabert, Louis. L’impasee Turque. Études, v. 170, 20
mars 1922: 670-698.   AP20.E8, v. 170

530
Jalabert, Louis. Kamâl Atatürk, le père des Turcs.
Études, v. 237, 5 déc. 1938: 647-653. AP20.E8, v. 237

531
Jalabert, Louis. La Turquie nouvelle. Études, v. 230,
5 fév. 1937: 289-312.   AP20.E8, v. 230

532
Jameson, Samuel H. Social mutation in Turkey.
Social forces, v. 14, May 1936: 482-496.
                                        HN51.S5, v. 14

533
Jamieson, Alan. Kemal Ataturk, 1881-1938. *In his*
Leaders of the twentieth century. London, Bell,
1970. p. 29-57.   D412.7.J3

534
Janeway, Eliot. Turkey becomes a world power. Travel, v. 71, Sept. 1938: 4-8.   G149.T73, v. 71

535
Jarman, Thomas L. Turkey. London, Arrowsmith, 1935. 132 p.   DR441.J3

536
Jarring, Gunnar V. Det nya Turkiet. Stockholm, Alb. Bonnier, 1937. 64 p.

537
Jarring, Gunnar V. Turkiet i farozonen. Stockholm, Kooperativa förbundets bokforlag, 1941. 32 p.   DR589.J35

538
Jarring, Gunnar V. Turkisk ungdomsuppfostran och Turkisk nationalism. Svensk tidskrift, v. 25. no. 7, 1938: 569-579.   AP48.S76, v. 25

539
Johnson, Stowers, Turkish panorama. London, Hale, 1968. 192 p.   DR429.J6

540
Jones, D. D., *and* Henry Johnson. Mustapha Kemal and Peter the Great: a study in parallelism. Sociology and social research, v. 22, Jan. 1938: 212-222.   HM1.S75, v. 22

541
Jones, E. Stanley. The meaning of the revolution in Turkey. Moslem world, v. 16, July 1926: 253-261.   DS36.M7, v. 16

542
Jonquiere, A. de la. Angora et Moscou. L'Asie française, v. 24, sept.-oct. 1924: 333-340.   JV1801.A85, v. 24

543
Jonquière, A. de la. Les reformes d'Angora. L'Asie française, v. 24, avril 1924: 148-152.   JV1801.A85, v. 24

544
Juncker-Jensen, Jens. Tyrkiet. En illustreret rejseforer. København, Gad. 1966. 159 p.   DR416.J8

545
Kabulśkiĭ, S. Politika vozrozdennoĭ Turĭsii. Mezhdunarodnaia zhizń, no. 7, 1926: 18-27.   D410.M4, no. 7

546
Kabulśkiĭ, S. Sovremennaia Turĭsiia. Mezhdunarodniia zhizń, no. 3, 1925: 27-44.   D410.M4, no. 3

547
Kaĭzo, N. Éksport sovetskogo sakhara v Turĭsiiu. Torgovliâ SSSR s vostokom, no. 1-2, ianv.-fevr., 1930: 23-30.   HC331.T58, no. 1-2

548
Kaloussis, D. Der Griechisch-Türkische Bevölkerungsaustausch in den Jahren 1922-1923. Leipzig, Verlag Gustav Fock, 1936. 68 p.

549
Kanellopoulos, K. D. Hē Mikrasiatikē ēta; Augostos 1922. Athēnai, 1936. 331 p.

550
Karabuda, Barbro. Anklagelser. Politiska reportage fran dagens Turkiet. Stockholm, Solna, 1970. 189 p.   DR590.K33

551
Karabuda, Barbro. Rosenkullen. Sanna berättelser fran Turkiet. Stockholm, Bonnier, 1966. 114 p.   DR432.K285

552
Karpat, Kemal H. The people's Houses in Turkey; establishment and growth. The Middle East journal, v. 17, Winter/Spring 1963: 55-67.   DS1.M5, v. 17

553
Karpat, Kemal H. Society, economics and politics in contemporary Turkey. World politics, v. 17, Oct. 1964: 50-74.   D839.W57, v. 17

554
Karpat, Kemal H. Turkey's politics; the transition to a multi-party system. Princeton, N. J., Princeton University Press, 1959. 522 p.   JN9798.A1K3

555
Kassimoff, Kassim. La Russie et les détroits. Lagny, E. Grevin, 1926. 140 p.   DR741.B7K3

556
Kayser, Jacques. A propos de la victoire turque.

L'Europe nouvelle, v. 5, 30 sept. 1922: 1234.

AP20.E88, v. 5

557

Kayser, Jacques. L'Europe et la Turquie nouvelle. Paris, Editions des Presses Universitaires de France. 1922. 137 p.   D463.K3

558

Kazamias, Andreas M. Education and the quest for modernity in Turkey. London, Allen & Unwin, 1966. 304 p.   LA941.K3

559

Kazimirskiĭ, G. K. Sovremennai͡a Evropeĭskai͡a Turtsii͡a. Novyi vostok, no. 16-17, 1927: 178-189.

YUDIN JN18.N9, no. 16-17

560

Keeler, Erwin P. Turkish budget for 1929-'30. *In* U.S. Bureau of Foreign and Domestic Commerce. Commerce reports, no. 35, Sept. 2, 1929: 637.

HC1.R21, no. 35

561

Kelly, Howard. A brief sketch of the policy of the Turkish republic. *In* Royal Central Asian Society. Journal, v. 32, July-Oct. 1945: 248-257.   DS1.R6, v. 32

562

Kemal Atatürk, Mustafa, 1881-1938. *In* Encyclopedia Britannica. Chicago, Encyclopedia Britannica, Inc. 1972, v. 13, p. 276-277.   AE5.E363

563

Kemal Ataturk politely emulates Hitler on treaties. Newsweek, v. 7, Apr. 25, 1936: 17.   AP2.N6772, v. 7

564

Kemal i ego druzi͡a. *In* Russia (1917-R.S.F.S.R.). Narodnoyi komissariat po inostrannym. Bi͡ulleten, no. 25, 5 ii͡ul 1920: 35-36.   D411.R92, no. 25

565

Kemal-pasha-diktator. *In* Russia (1917-R.S.F.S.R.). Narodnoyi komissariat po inostrannym delam. Bi͡ulleten, no. 29, 20 avg. 1920: 45-46.

D411.R92, no. 29

566

Kemal-pasha i korol Konstantin. *In* Russia (1917-R.S.F.S.R.). Narodnoyi komissariat po inostrannym delam. Bi͡ulleten, no. 54, 31 dek. 1920: 3-4.

D411.R92, no. 54

567

Kemal Pasha's summit of achievement. Literary digest, v. 79, Nov. 17, 1923: 21-22.   AP2.L58, v. 79

568

Mme. Kemal tells of her romantic marriage to the Turkish president. Current opinion, v. 76, Jan. 1924: 79-80.   AP2.C95, v. 76

569

Kemal's third term. Literary digest, v. 109, May 16, 1931: 16.   AP2.L58, v. 109

570

Kemalisty i antanta. *In* Russia (1917-R.S.F.S.R.). Narodnoyi komissariat po inostrannym delam. Biulleten, no. 91, 10 sent. 1921: 61-62.   D411.R92, no. 91

571

Kemalisty i Islam. Bi͡ulleten pressy srednogo vostoka, no. 1, sent. 1929: 29-32.   DS1.B5, no. 1

572

Kemalisty ob angliĭskoĭ politike. *In* Russia (1917-R.S.F.S.R.). Narodnoyi komissariat po inostrannym delam. Bi͡ulleten, no. 78, 5 ii͡un 1921: 33-34.

D411.R92, no. 78

573

Kemalisty ustupuli strategicheskiĭ platsdarm. Bi͡ulleten pressy srednego vostoka, no. 3, noi͡abr 1929: 77-78.   DS1.B5, no. 3

574

Kerekeshàzy, Jòzsef. Az i Gazi Kemàl; egy köztàrsasàg születèse. Budapest, Pantheon, 1943. 302 p.

575

Kerner, Robert J. Social sciences in the Balkans and in Turkey. Berkeley, University of California Press, 1930. 137 p.   H65.K4

576

Kerner, Robert J. *and* Harry N. Howard. The Balkan conferences and the Balkan entente, 1930-1935; a study in the recent history of the Balkan and Near Eastern peoples. Berkeley, Calif., University of California Press, 1936. 271 p.   D463.K4

577

Khanki, Aziz. Turcs et Atatürk. Le Caire, Imp. F. E. Noury et fils, 1939. 188 p.   DR589.K415

578

Kılıç, Altemur. Turkey and the world. Washington, D. C., Public Affairs Press, 1959. 224 p.   DR590.K5

579
Kiazim, Omer (Kâzım Ömer). Angora et Berlin; le complot germano-kemaliste contre le traité de Versailles. Paris, l'Édition Universelle, 1922. 174 p.

580
Kiazim, Omer (Kâzım, Ömer) L'aventure Kemaliste; elle est un danger: pour l'Orient, pour l'Europe, pour la paix. Paris, l'Édition Universelle, 1921. 104 p.   DR589.K52

581
Kienitz, Friedrich K. Türkei; Anschluss und die moderne Wirtschaft unter Kemal Ataturk. Hamburg, 1959. 148 p.

582
Kili, Suna. Kemalism. Istanbul, Robert College, 1969. 239 p.   DR590.K48

583
Kili, Suna. Turkey: a case study of political development. Istanbul, Robert College, 1968. 44 p.
                                                DR442.K53

584
King, Eric H. Tourist in the Turkish capitals of Anatolia. Asiatic review, v. 34, Jan. 1938: 107-111.
                                                DS1.A7, v. 34

585
Kinross, John P., *baron.* Ataturk; a biography of Mustafa Kemal, father of modern Turkey. New York, Morrow, 1965. 615 p.   DR592.K4K43

586
Kinross, John P., *baron.* Atatürk, the rebirth of a nation. London, Weidenfeld & Nicolson, 1964. 542 p.   DR589.K54

587
Kinross, John P., *baron.* Europa Minor, journeys in coastal Turkey. London, Murray, 1956. 167 p.
                                                DR428.K5

588
Kinross, John P., *baron.* Within the Taurus; a journey in Asiatic Turkey. New York, Morrow, 1955. 191 p.   DS49.3.K48

589
Kitaĭgorodskiĭ, P. Oktiabrskaia revoliutsiia i natsionalno-revoliutsionne dvizhenie Turt͡sii.
Krasnaia internat͡sional profsoiuzov, no. 10, 1927: 407-411.   HD6475.A2R34, no. 10

590
Kitaĭgorodskiĭ, P. Turt͡siia. Moskva, Izd-vo Tsk Mopr SSSR, 1929. 32 p.

591
Kitaĭgorodskiĭ, P. Turt͡siia i agressiyĭ Italĭânskiĭ imperializm. Bolshevik, no. 9-10, 30 maĭ 1926: 71-76.   HX8.K56, no. 9-10

592
Kitaĭgorodskiĭ, P. Zametki o Kemalistskoĭ Turt͡sii. Bolshevik, no. 18, 30 sent. 1927: 41-50.
                                                HX8.K56, no. 18

593
Kitapçı, Tahsin. L'histoire monétaire de la Turquie. Dijon, Imprimerie Bernigaud et Privat, 1939. 109 p.   HG1162.K55

594
Klinghardt, Karl. Angora-Konstantinopel. Frankfurt am Main, Frankfurter societätsdruckerei, 1924. 265 p.   DR589.K6

595
Klinghardt, Karl. Türkün jordu, der Türken heimatland, eine geographisch-politische landesschilderung. Hamburg, L. Friederichsen, 1925. 177 p.
                                                DS49.3.K5

596
Klinghardt, Karl. Zehn jahre unter dem Gazi. Berlin, Wilhelm Kronecker, 1934. 185 p.

597
Kohn, Hans. The Turkish revolution. *In his* Revolutions and dictatorships. Cambridge, Mass., Harvard University Press, 1941. p. 249-277.   D720.K6

598
Kohn, Hans. Ten years of the Turkish republic. Foreign affairs, v. 12, Oct. 1933: 141-155.
                                                D410.F6, v. 12

599
Koldjako, L. S. Ekonomocheskaia zhizn Anatolii. Novyi vostok, no. 4, 1923: 230-249.
                                                JUDIN JN18.N9, no. 4

600
Kornienko, Radmir P. Rabochee dvizhenie v Turt͡sii, 1918-1963 gg. Moskva, Nauk, 1965. 173 p.
                                                HD8616.K6

601
Korolkova. Latinskiĭ alfavit v Turt͡sii. Novyi vostok,
no. 13/14, 1923: 457-458. YUDIN JN18.N9, no. 13/14

602
Kostól, Sigmun S. Tyrkia sett med egne óyne. Oslo,
Green, 1968. 140 p.   DR429.K6

603
Kral, August. Atatürk, kleine Biographie. Berliner
monatshefte, v. 17, März 1939: 193-225.
                              D511.A1B4, v. 17·

604
Kral, August. Das land Kamâl Atatürks; der werde-
gang der modernen Türkei. Wien-Leipzig, W.
Braumüller, 1937. 344 p.   DR589.K66

605
Krehel, Peter. Constitutions in the making: Turkey,
sick man in a sick world. Common sense, v. 4, Aug.
1950: 38-41.   JX1901.C68, v. 4

606
Kreider, Herman H., *and* Maynard O. Williams.
Looking in on new Turkey; with colored photographs. National geographic magazine, v. 62, Apr.
1932: 499-508.   G1.N27, v. 62

607
Kross, T. Vnutrennee polozhenie Turt͡sii. Mezhdu-
narodnaiâ zhizń, no. 7-8, 1930: 57-66.
                              D410.M4, no. 7-8

608
Krüger, Karl. Kemalist Turkey and the Middle East.
London, George Allen, 1932. 233 p.   DR589.K7

609
Krüger, Karl. Die Türkei. Berlin, Safari, 1951. 392 p.
                              DR417.K78

610
Kurczewski, Mieczyslaw. Turcja. Warszawa, Wojskowy Instytut Geograficny, 1936. 125 p.

611
Kurtoğlu, Faik. La Turquie vous offre le marché
qu'il vous faut. Bruxelles, Imprimeur du roi, 1932.
134 p.   HC405.K8

612
Kuznet͡sova, S. I. Ustanovlenie Sovetsko-Turet͡skikh
otnoshenii. Moskva, Izd. Vost. Lit., 1961. 85 p.

613
Labonne, Roger. Les origines du mouvement nation-
aliste Turc. Revue de Paris, v. 29, 1 oct. 1922:
477-501.   AP20.R27, v. 29

614
Lachs, Otto. Kemal Atatürk; Leben und Werk in
Bildern. Leipzig, Erich Kalis, 1939. 112 p.

615
Ladas, Stephen P. Exchange of minorities; Bulgaria,
Greece and Turkey. New York, Macmillan, 1932.
849 p.   D650.T4L2

616
Lahanokardos, Evangelos. Neon apleton phõs eis
tēn Mikrasiatikin katastrophēn kai ho Gen. Lufas.
Athēnai, Etniki Ora, 1928. 137 p.

617
Lamontagne, Yves. Trade and industrial notes on
Turkey. *In* Canada. Dept. of Trade and Commerce.
Commercial intelligence journal, v. 53, Nov. 16,
1935: 864-867.   HF129.A27, v. 53

618
Lamouche, Léon. Histoire de la Turquie depuis les
origines jusqu'à nos jours. Paris, Payot, 1934. 427 p.
                              DR440.L33

619
Lamour, Philippe. L'influence française en Turquie
et les frères des écoles chrétiennes. Revue politique
et parlementaire, v. 117, nov. 1923: 216-333.
                              H3.R4, v. 117

620
Landen, Robert G. *comp.* The emergence of the modern Middle East. New York, Van Nostrand Rein-
hold Co., 1970. 366 p.   DS62.4L3

621
Lane, Winthrop D. Why Greeks and Turks oppose
being "exchanged". Current history, v. 18, Apr.
1923: 86-90.   D410.C8, v. 18

622
Langley, Michael P. Ankara, Turkey's new capital.
Travel, v. 66, Apr. 1936: 16-19.   G149.T73, v. 66

623
Langley, Michael P. Social reforms in Turkey. Contemporary review, v. 147, May 1935: 566-573.
                              AP4.C7, v. 147

624
Langley, Michael P. Turkey awakes. Living age, v. 349, Dec. 1935: 339-342.   AP2.L65, v. 349

625
Langley, Michael P. Turkey's new capital. Geographical magazine, v. 1, Sept. 1935: 340-355.
          G1.G343, v. 1

626
Langsam, Walter C. Turkey for the Turks; from Sèvres to Lausanne. *In his* The world since 1919. New York, Macmillan, 1971. p. 233-242.   D720.L27

627
Lassus Saint-Geniès, Odile de. Vacances en Turquie. Paris, l'Inter, 1966. 160 p.   DR416.L3

628
Latimer, Frederick P. The political philosophy of Mustapha Kemal Atatürk as evidenced in his published speeches and interviews. Ann Arbor, University of Michigan Press, 1963. 229 p.

629
Latouche, M. B. La Turquie après quinze ans de Kemalisme. L'Asie française, v. 36, avril 1936: 108-113.
          JV1801.A85, v. 36

630
Lausanne and the freedom of the Straits. Economist, v. 95, Dec. 9, 1922: 1064-1065.   HG11.E2, v. 95

631
Lausanne and Sèvres. Economist, v. 96, Feb. 10, 1923: 252-253.   HG11.E2, v. 96

632
The Lausanne conference. Round table, v. 13, Mar. 1923: 342-355.   AP4.R6, v. 13

633
The Lausanne treaty. Atlantic monthly, v. 134, Nov. 1924:693-700.   AP2.A8, v. 134

634
Lavrov, Nikolaĭ M. Turt͡siia v 1918-1956 godakh; uchebiyĭ material. Moskva, Vyssharia partiĭnaia shkola pri Tsk KPSS, 1956. 52 p.   DR590.L3

635
Lebeau, Charles-Hippolyte. Essai sur la justice en Turquie (à propos du traité de Lausanne). Paris, Marcel Rivière, 1924. 123 p.   D462 1923 m

636
Lee, Rose. Social swim in Angora. Century, v. 113, Jan. 1927: 317-325.   AP2.C4, v. 113

637
Lee, Rose. When Mustapha Kemal dances; the social flowering of the republican capital at Angora. World today, v. 49, Apr. 1927: 451-457.
          AP4.W85, v. 49

638
Lemercier, Camille. La tâche difficile du nouveau gouvernement turc. L'Europe nouvelle, v. 7, 18 oct. 1924: 1392-1394.   AP20.E88, v. 7

639
Lenczowski, George. The Middle East in world affairs. Ithaca, N.Y., Cornell University Press, 1962. 723 p.   DS62.L53

640
Lengyel, Emil. They called him Ataturk. New York, John Day, 1962. 192 p.   DR592.K4L4

641
Lengyel, Emil. Turkey. New York, Random house, 1941. 474 p.   DR440.L4

642
Levonian, Lutfi. The Turkish press; selections from the Turkish press showing events and opinions, 1925-1932, translated and arranged under direction of Lutfi Levonian. Athens, School of Religion, 1932. 216 p.

643
Lévy, Roger. Constantinople. L'Europe nouvelle, v. 5, 23 sept. 1922: 1187-1188.   AP20.E88, v. 5

644
Lewis, Bernard. The emergence of modern Turkey. New York, Oxford University Press, 1968. 530 p.
          DR583.L48

645
Lewis, Bernard. Islamic revival in Turkey. International affairs, v. 28, Jan. 1952: 38-48.
          JX1.I53, v. 28

646
Lewis, Bernard. Turkey today. London, Hutchinson, 1940. 127 p.   DR589.L47

647
Lewis, Geoffrey L. Turkey. 2d rev. ed. New York, Praeger, 1960. 226 p.   DR441.L45

648
Lewis, Geoffrey L. Turkey: the end of the first republic. World today, v. 16, Sept. 1960: 377-386.
          AP4.W85, v. 16

649
Lewis, Geoffrey L. Turkey: the thorny road to democracy. World today, v. 18, May 1962: 182-191.
          AP4.W85, v. 18

650
Lewis, Herbert. Anatolien. Geographische zeitschrift, v. 45, Nov. 1939: 353-376.   G1.G37, v. 45

651
Liais, Michel. La conférence de Lausanne. Revue générale de droit international public, v. 40, jan.-fév. 1933: 71-89.   JX3.R56, v. 40

652
Lierau, Walter. Die neue Türkei; wirtschaftliche Zustände und Aussichten. Berlin, E. S. Mittler, 1923. 59 p.   HC405.L46

653
Linke, Lilo. Allah dethroned; a journey through modern Turkey. London, Constable, 1937. 341 p.
          DR428.L5

654
Linke, Lilo. Social changes in Turkey; with discussion. International affairs, v. 16, July 1937: 540-563.
          JX1.153, v. 16

655
Lister, Richard P. Turkey observed. London, Eyre & Spottiswoode, 1967. 271 p.   DR429.L5

656
Lium, Rolf. Kemal, a play in three acts. Istanbul, 1966. 173 p.   PR6062.I87K4

657
Loewenthal, Rudolf. Russian materials on Turkey; a selective bibliography. Washington, Dept. of State, External Research Staff, Office of Intelligence Research, 1958. 19 p.   JX231.A3 no. 133.4

658
Loiseau, Charles. Un ferry-boat sur le Bosphore. Le monde slave, v. 1, mars 1935: 344-356.
          D461.M7, v. 1

659
Lord Curzon and the Turks. Economist, v. 97, Oct. 13, 1923: 548-550.   HG11.E2, v. 13

660
Lore, Ludwig. Turkey: a new world power. Jewish frontier, v. 5, Sept. 1938: 12-15.   DS149.A324, v. 5

661
Ludshuveit, Evgenii F. Sovremennoe polozhenie turetskikh prolivov. Novyi vostok, no. 23/24, 1928: 292-303.   JUDIN JN18.N9, no. 23/24

662
Ludshuveit, Evgenii F. Turtsiia; zkonomiko-geograficheskii ocherk. Moskva, Gos. izd-vo geogr. lit-ry, 1955. 397 p.   HC405.L8

663
Ludwig, Emil. The creator of a state. Sphere, v. 122, Sept. 13, 1930: 460-461, 480.   AP4.S73, v. 122

664
Luke, Sir Harry C. Angora language reform. Quarterly review, v. 264, Jan. 1935: 65-72. AP4.Q2, v. 264

665
Luke, Sir Harry C. The making of modern Turkey: from Byzantium to Angora. London, Macmillan, 1936. 246 p.   DR440.L8

666
Lyautey, Pierre. Turquie moderne. Paris, Julliard, 1970. 280 p.   DR417.L96

667
Lybyer, Albert H. "Constantinople" or "Mustafa Kemal". Current history, v. 26, Aug. 1927: 828-829.
          D410.C8, v. 26

668
Lybyer, Albert H. Modern Turkey. Chicago, Open Court Publishers, 1932. 180 p.   OCU
          ABBS

669
Lybyer, Albert H. The political reconstruction of Turkey. Open court, v. 46, May 1932: 306-319.
          AP2.0495, v. 46

670
Lybyer, Albert H. Reform of Turkish education.
Current history, v. 37, Oct. 1932: 119-120.
D410.C8, v. 37

671
Lybyer, Albert H. The return of the Turk. Forum,
v. 69, May 1923: 1544-1552.   AP2.F8, v. 69

672
Lybyer, Albert H. Turkey and the Near East. Cur-
rent history, v. 25, Mar. 1927: 935-936.
D410.C8, v. 25

673
Lychowski, Tadeusz. Turcja; rys stosunkow geograf-
icznych, gospodarczych, politycnych i wojskowych.
Warszawa, Wojskowy Instytut Naukowo-Wydawn-
iczy, 1924. 80 p.   DR589.L8

674
MacCallum, Elizabeth P., *and* Earle, Edward M. Turkey's coming of age. Asia, v. 26, July 1927: 585-589,
654-659.   HF3119.A5, v. 26

675
MacCallum, Frank L. Turkey discovers the Koran.
Moslem world, v. 23, Jan. 1933: 24-28.
DS36.M7, v. 23

676
McCally, Sarah P. Party government in Turkey; development of political parties. Journal of politics,
v. 18, May 1956: 297-323.   JA1.J6, v. 18

677
McDowell, Edward C., Jr. Dardanelles; explaining
their refortification in the foreboding light of
history. Current history, v. 45, Nov. 1936: 92-96.
D410.C8, v. 45

678
McGhee, George C. Turkey joins the West; transformation of the country in the last few decades. Foreign affairs, v. 32, July 1954: 617-630.
D410.F6, v. 32

679
Marcario, Gianni B. Notizie sulla campagna Turca-
Greca 1919-1922. Rivista militare Italiana, v. 5,
nov. 1931: 1669-1704, dic. 1931: 1891-1926.
U4.R57, v. 5

680
Macartney, Maxwell H. Angora and the Caliphate.
Fortnightly review, v. 121, Apr. 1924: 495-505.
AP4.F7, v. 121

681
Macartney, Maxwell H. The new Grand Assembly.
Fortnightly review, v. 120, Nov. 1923: 742-751.
AP4.F7, v. 120

682
Macartney, Maxwell H. The new opposition in Tur-
key. Fortnightly review, v. 123, June 1925: 781-793.
AP4.F7, v. 123

683
Macartney, Maxwell H. Turkey in revolution. Fort-
nightly review, v. 124, Nov. 1925: 652-653.
AP4.F7, v. 124

684
Macartney, R. H. Ankara, the capital of modern Tur-
key. Builder, v. 152, June 4, 1937: 1171-1174.
NA1.B5, v. 152

685
Mackenzie, Albert. Crimes of Turkish misrule. Cur-
rent history, v. 17, Oct. 1922: 28-31.
D410.C8, v. 17

686
Mackie, G. B. Turkish industrialization. *In* Royal
Central Asian Society. Journal, v. 26, July 1939:
440-453.   DS1.R6, v. 26

687
Maclean, Fitzroy. The Eastern question in modern
dress. Foreign affairs, v. 29, Jan. 1951: 238-247.
D410.F6, v. 29

688
Mamopoulos, P. La question des Détroits. Les Balkans, v. 4, mai-juin 1933; 37-41.   DR1.B35, v. 4

689
Mango, Andrew. Turkey. New York, Walker, 1968.
192 p.   DR590.M35

690
Mantran, Robert. Histoire de la Turquie. Paris,
Presses universitaires de France, 1968. 128 p.
DR441.M35

691
Mantran, Robert. Turkey. Paris, Hachette, 1955.
126 p.   DR722.M35

692

Marchand, René. Le réveil d'une race; dans la Turquie de Mustapha Kemal. Paris, La Nouvelle société d'édition, 1927. 229 p.   DR589.M3

693

Marcosson, Isaac F. Kemal Ataturk. *In* Fernsworth, Lawrence A. *ed.* Dictators and democrats. New York, R. M. McBride, 1941. p. 227-250.   D412.6.F45

694

Marcosson, Isaac F. Kemal Pasha. Saturday evening post, v. 196, Oct. 20, 1923: 8-9, 141.   AP2.S2, v. 196

695

Marcu, Valeriu. Kemal Pascha oder von der nationalen farce zur nationalen Revolution. *In his* Männer und Mächte der Gegenwart. Berlin, G. Kiepenheuer, 1930: p. 127-152.   D412.M3

696

Mariner, John. Journey into the sunrise. London, William Kimber, 1970. 253 p.   DR429.M35

697

Martinescu, A. Th. Lenin, Benito Mussolini, Mustafa Kemal. Bucuresti, 1930. 136 p.

698

Martino, Perrone di San F. Un dittatore asiatico: Mustafà Kemal il vittorioso. Torino, Casa Editrice F. Casanova, 1930. 217 p.

699

Marvin, George. The Greek military débâcle. Asia, v. 22, Dec. 1922: 957-1006.   HF3119.A5, v. 22

700

Mary-Rousselière, André. La Turquie constitutionelle, contribution à l'étude de la politique interieure Turque. Rennes, Imp. Réunies, 1925. 359 p.

701

Marzio, Cornelio di. La Turchia di Kemal. Milano, Casa editrice "Alpes", 1926. 326 p.   DR589.M33

702

Mason, Shirley L. Geology of prospective oil territory in Republic of Turkey. American association of petroleum geologists-bulletin, v. 14, June 1930: 687-704.   TN860.A3, v. 14

703

Massigli, René L. La Turquie devant la guerre; mission à Ankara, 1939-1940. Paris, Plon, 1964. 511 p.   DR592.A1M3

704

Masterman, Charles F. The return of the Turk. Atlantic monthly, v. 131, Jan. 1923: 106-115.   AP2.A8, v. 131

705

Maurer, Renate. Briefe aus Anatolien. Bern, Bargezzi, 1967. 85 p.   DR432.M42

706

Mears, Eliot G. Modern Turkey; a politico-economic interpretation, 1908-1923 inclusive, with selected chapters by representative authorities. New York, Macmillan, 1924. 779 p.   DR578.M4

707

Medriczky, Andor. Kemál Atatürk a hadvezér, az allamférfi és az ember. Turán, v. 20-21, 1937-1938: 121-138.   DS1.T8, v. 20-21

708

Melamid, Alexander. Turkey. Garden City, N. Y., N. Doubleday, 1967. 64 p.   DR418.M38

709

Mêlia, Jean. Mustapha Kémal, ou la rénovation de la Turquie. Paris, Bibliothèque-Charpontier, 1929. 240 p.   DR592.M8M4

710

Mel'nik, A. Ekonomicheskiĭ krizis v Turt͡sii. Mezhdunarodnai͡a zhisn', no. 1, 1930: 37-56.   D410.M4, no. 1

711

Mel'nik, A. Franko-Turet͡skiĭ konflikt. Mezhdunarodnai͡a zhizn', no. 1, 1929: 42-53.   D410.M4, no. 1

712

Mel'nik, A. Greko-Turet͡ski raznoglasii͡a. Mezhdunarodnai͡a zhizn', no. 8, 1929: 55-67.   D410.M4, no. 8

713

Mel'nik, A. Novai͡a partii͡a v Turt͡sii. Mezhdunarodnai͡a zhisn', no. 9/10, 1930: 3-19.   D410.M4, no. 9/10

714

Mel'nik, A. Pi͡at let v respublikanskos Turt͡sii. Mezhdunarodnai͡a zhizn', no. 11, 1928: 3-11.   D410.M4, no. 11

715
Mel'nik, A. Turt͡siia. Moskva, Sotsekgiz, 1937. 216 p.
DR418.M4

716
Melzig, Herbert. Kemâl Atatürk; üntergang und Aufstieg der Türkei. Frankfurt a. M., Societätsverlag, 1937. 293 p.
DR592.K4M43

717
Merriam, Gordon P. Regional geography: Anatolia. Economic geography, v. 2, Jan. 1926: 87-107.
HF1021.E4, v. 2

718
Merrill, Frederick T. Twelve years of the Turkish republic. Foreign policy reports, v. 11, Oct. 9, 1935: 190-200.
D410.F65, v. 11

719
Mestre, Achille. L'étranger en Turquie d'après le Traité de Lausanne. Revue politique et parlementaire, v. 116, 10 août 1923: 179-206.
H3.R4, v. 116

720
Meyering, H. R. The Turkish stereotype. Sociology and social research, v. 22, Nov. 1937: 112-123.
HM1.S75, v. 22

721
Michailidēs, K. Hē katastrophē kai hoi telentaies hēmeres tēs Smyrnēs. Athēnai, 1925. 47 p.

722
Migliorini, Elio. La nuova Turchia: viaggi e scritti recenti. Bolletino della società geografica Italiana, v. 73, ott., 1936: 589-621.
G17.S67, v. 73

723
Mihajlović, Dragoslav P. La nouvelle Turquie économique. Beograd, Institut Balkanique, 1937. 171 p.
HC405.M515

724
Mikusch, Dagobert. Gasi Mustafà Kemal, zwischen Europa und Asien. Leipzig, P. List, 1929. 340 p.
DR592.K4M5

725
Mikusch, Dagobert and Béla Horváth. Kemál Atatürk; Gázi Musztafa Kemál; fél évszázad Törökország történtéböl. Budapest, Béla Horváth, 1937. 199 p.

726
Miller, Anatoliĭ F. Chanakskiĭ krizis i vopros o prolivakh. Moskva, 1966. 20 p.
DR477.M5

727
Miller, Anatoliĭ F. Kratkai͡a istorii͡a Turt͡sii. Moskva, Gos. Izd-vo polit. Lit-ry, 1948. 303 p.
DR441.M63

728
Miller, Anatoliĭ F. Ocherki noveĭsheĭ Turt͡sii. Moskva, Izd-vo, Akademii Nauk SSSR, 1948. 279 p.
DR590.M5

729
Miller, Anatoliĭ F. Turt͡siia i problema prolivov. Moskva, Pravda, 1947. 23 p.
D372.M5

730
Miller, Barnette. The new Turkey. In American Academy of Political and Social Science. Annals, v. 108, July 1923: 132-140.
H1.A4, v. 108

731
Miller, John L., and Mrs. Madeleine S. Miller. Dardanelles, straits of destiny. Travel, v. 75, July 1940: 32-35.
G149.T73, v. 75

732
Miller, William. The Greco-Turkish friendship. Contemporary review, v. 140, Dec. 1931: 718-726.
AP4.C7, v. 140

733
Miller, William. The Ottoman empire and its successors, 1801-1927, with an appendix, 1927-1936. Cambridge (Eng.), University press, 1936. 644 p.
DR557.M6

734
Miller, William. The return of the Turks. Quarterly review, v. 242, Oct. 1924: 334-345.
AP4.Q2, v. 242

735
Mohr, Paul. Konstantinopel und die Merrengenfrage. Berlin, Paul Vohwinckel Verlag, 1927. 95 p.
DR731.M6

736
Moiseev, Petr P. Turt͡siia. Moskva, Mysl', 1965. 156 p.
HC405.M6

737
Moiseev, Petr P., *and* Iu. K. Rozaliev. K istorii
Sovotsko-Turetskikh otnosheniĭ. Moskva, Gospo-
litzdat, 1958. 84 p.

738
Money for guns: Turkey refortifying Dardanelles.
Literary digest, v. 122, Aug. 1, 1936: 14.
AP2.L58, v. 122

739
Montgomery, George R. Turkey and the Americans.
Current history, v. 17, Nov. 1922: 303-305.
D410.C8, v. 17

740
Monty. T. J. Trade of Turkey in 1931. *In* Canada.
Dept. of Trade and Commerce. Commercial intel-
ligence journal, v. 46, June 18, 1932: 1061-1063.
HF129.A27, v. 46

741
Mood, James R. Turko-Greek repatriation, a serious
problem. *In* U.S. Bureau of Foreign and Domestic
Commerce. Commerce reports, no. 43, Oct. 27,
1924: 211-213.
HC1.R21, no. 43

742
Moore, Lawrence S. New Turkey of Mustapha Kemal.
Asia, v. 22, Apr. 1922: 302-310.
HF3119.A5, v. 22

743
Mr. Morgenthau protests. Outlook, v. 143, June 2,
1926: 163-164.
AP2.O8, v. 143

744
Móricz, Péter. Gázi Musztafa Kemál és a Török köz-
társaság alkotásai. Turán, v. 16, 1933: 7-15.
DS1.T8, v. 16

745
Morrison, Charles C. Rebirth of a nation. Christian
century, v. 52, June 12, 1935: 785-786.
BR1.C45, v. 52

746
Morrison, Charles C. Religion in Turkey. Christian
century, v. 52, July 3, 1935: 880-881.
BR1.C45, v. 52

747
Morrison, Charles C. Should missionaries remain in
Turkey? Christian century, v. 52, July 17, 1935:
935-937.
BR1.C45, v. 52

748
Morrison, Charles C. Turkey's dictator. Christian
century, v. 52, June 26, 1935: 847-849.
BR1.C45, v. 52

749
Morrison, Charles C. Turkey's predicament. Chris-
tian century, v. 52, June 19, 1935: 816-818.
BRI.C45, v. 52

750
Morrison, S. A. Religious liberty in Turkey. International review of missions, v. 24, Oct. 1935:
441-459.
BV2351.I6, v. 24

751
Moschopulos, Nikephoros. Le despotisme éclairé en
Turquie. Paris, Les Presses Universitaires de
France. 1937. 35 p.

752
Moses, Kingsley. The crescent rises; will the Turk
penetrate Italian Tripoli? Outlook, v. 132, Nov. 1,
1922: 371-374.
AP2.O8, v. 132

753
Mosharrafa, Moustafa M. Ataturk, a biography.
Cairo, Anglo-Egyptian Bookshop, 1944. 202 p.
DR592.K4M7

754
A Moslem revolution. Youth's companion, v. 96, Dec.
7, 1922: 706.
AP201.Y8, v. 96

755
Moss, Arthur, *and* Florence Gilliam. The Turkish
myth. Nation, v. 116, June 13, 1923: 704-705.
AP2.N2, v. 116

756
Mostras, Basileios D. Hē Mikrasiatikē epicheirēsis.
Athēnai, Ikaros, 1969. 81 p.
DF845.M65

757
Mourão, Gerardo M. Mustafa Kemal. Rio de Janeiro,
Norte editora, 1938. 58 p.
DR592.K4M42

758
Mousset, Albert. Montreux et la question des Détroits. L'Europe nouvelle, v. 19, 27 juin 1936:
663-665.
AP20.E88, v. 19

759
Moutal, Mosché S. L'avenir économique de la Tur-

quie nouvelle. Paris, Librairie Jouve, 1925. 156 p.
MH

760
Mu'ammar Wassaf. Die grundlinien des türkischen Staatswesens und seine ·stufenweise Entwicklung. Leipzig, R. Noske, 1934. 98 p. JN9711.M8

761
Musalli. Ekonomicheskaia konferentsia v Smirne. Novyi vostok, no. 3, 1923: 78-89.
YUDIN JN18.N9, no. 3

762
Musil, Alois, Most do Asie; nové Turecko. Praha, Melantrich, 1941. 262 p.

763
Mustafa Kemal. Contemporary review, v. 122, Nov. 1922: 590-594. AP4.C7, v. 122

Signed: J. G. B.

764
Mustapha Kemal as arbiter of Turkey's fate. Current history, v. 19, Mar. 1924: 1040-1043.
D410.C8, v. 19

765
Mustafa Kemal' i Konstantinopolskoe pravitelstvo. In Russia (1917-R.S.F.S.R.). Narodnoyi komissariat po inostrannym delam. Biulleten, no. 67, 5 mart 1921: 40-41. D411.R92, no. 67

766
Mustafa Kemal' prigovoren k smerti. In Russia (1917-R.S.F.S.R.). Narodnoyi komissariat po inostrannym delam. Biulleten, no. 19, 20 iiun 1920: 31.
D411.R92, no. 19

767
Muzaffar, Jamal. Terror of the Red Fox and reforms of the Grey Wolf. Washington, 1957. 42 p.
DR577.M87

768
Nach, James. Turkey in pictures. New York, Sterling, 1965. 64 p. DR418.N3

769
Nadolny, Rudolf. Zehn jahre Türkischer aussenpolitik. Europäische revue, v. 12, Juni 1936: 449-457.
AP30.E8, v. 12

770
Nahid, Hachim. Les symptômes de la crise turque et son remède. Paris, J. Vrin, 1931. 88 p. DR589.N3

771
Narodnoe prosveshchenie v Turtsii. Narodnoe prosveshchenie, no. 8, avg. 1926: 122-128.
L51.N32, no. 8

772
Nava, Santi. La questione del Hatay (Alessandretta) e la sua soluzione. Firenze, Studio Fiorentino di Politica Estera, 1939. 152 p. DS99.A57N3

773
Nava, Santi. Il regime degli Stretti Turchi dopo la guorra. Firenze, Studio Fiorentino di Politica Estera, 1937. 62 p. JX1393.S8N3

774
Nayman, Esma. Die stellung der frau in der neuen Türkei. Europäische revue, v. 12, Juni 1936: 506-512. AP30.E8, v. 12

775
Nazaroff, Alexander. Russia's treaty with Turkey. Current history, v. 17, Nov. 1922: 276-279.
D410.C8, v. 17

776
The Near East. Round table, v. 12, Mar. 1922: 319-337.
AP4.R6, v. 12

777
The Near East. Round table v. 13, Dec. 1922: 1-29.
AP4.R6, v. 13

778
Nelson, C. R. Kemalist Turkey and the Soviet Union, 1920-1926. M. A. thesis, Stanford University, Palo Alto, Calif. 1949.

779
Die neue Türkei. Istanbul, Druck und Verlag: Universum, 1936. 48 p. DR589.N4

780
The new Eastern question. Youth's companion, v. 96, Oct. 26, 1922: 612-613. AP201.Y8, v. 96

781
The new ruler of Turkey. Youth's companion, v. 96, Oct. 12, 1922: 584. AP201.Y8, v. 96

782
The new Turkey. Youth's companion, v. 97, Nov. 8, 1923: 674.   AP201.Y8, v. 97

783
New Turkish crisis. Current history, v. 17, Nov. 1922: 181-193.   D410.C8, v. 17

784
Newman, Bernard. Turkey and the Turks. London, Jenkins, 1968. 224 p.   DR429.N48

785
Newman, Bernard. Turkish crossroads. New York, Philosophical Library, 1952. 258 p.   DR428.N4

786
Newman, E. Polson. Italy, Greece and Turkey. Nineteenth century and after, v. 100, Oct. 1926: 545-555.
                                                  AP4.N7, v. 100

787
Nicol, E. Angora et la France. Paris, Société Générale d'Imprimerie et d'Editions, 1922. 36 p.   CSt-H

788
Nielsen, Svend A. En färd genom Dardanellerna och Bosporen. Jorden runt, v. 17, juni 1945: 378-388.
                                                  G149.J54. v. 17

789
Nilson, Paul E. Turkey seen from Tarsus. Moslem world, v. 14, Apr. 1924: 156-158.   DS36.M7, v. 14

790
Noordman, W. E. De ropubliek Turkije. Moppel, J. A. Boom, 1948. 214 p.   DR417.N65

791
Novichev, Aron D. Krest'iânstvo Turtsii v noveĭshee vremiâ. Moskva, Izd-vo vostochnoĭ lit-ry, 1959. 288 p.   HD805.N6

792
Novichev, Aron D. Turtsiiâ; kratkaiâ istoriiâ. Moskva, Nauka, 1965. 269 p.   DR441.N7

793
Nowack, Ernest. Journeys in northern Anatolia. Geographical review, v. 21, Jan. 1931: 70-92.
                                                  G1.G35, v. 21

794
Nute, Mary R. Village women in Turkey. World dominion, v. 11, Oct. 1933: 368-372.
                                                  BT2000.W6, v. 11

795
Obstinate new Turks. Outlook, v. 134, July 11, 1923: 355-357.   AP2.08, v. 134

796
Oeconomos, Lysimachos. The martyrdom of Smyrna and Eastern Christendom. London, George Allen & Unwin, 1922. 237 p.   DS51.S704

797
Ökçün, A. Gündüz. A guide to Turkish treaties (1920-1964). Ankara, Ankara Üniversitesi Basımevi, 1966. 248 p.   JY846.038

798
Östrupp, Johannes. Det nye Tyrki, Tyrkiest nyere historie dets politiske, ökonomiske og aandelige i vor tid. København, Udvalget for Folkeophysnings fremme, 1931. 256 p.

799
Oezbek, Sait Emin. La sümer bank et l'industrialization de la Turquie sous la république. Lyon, Imprimerie du Salut public, 1938. 181 p.   NN

800
Olivero, Luigi. Turchia senza harem. Roma, D. de Luigi, 1945. 131 p.   DR589.04

801
Orga, Irfan. Phoenix ascendant; the rise of modern Turkey. London, R. Hale, 1958. 205 p. DR592.K407

802
Orga, Irfan *and* Margarete Orga. Atatürk. London, M. Joseph, 1962. 304 p.   DR592.K4068

803
Osten, Necmi. Administrative organization of Turkey: historical summary and present day administration, central and local. Asiatic review, v. 38, Oct. 1942: 407-413.   DS1.A7, v. 38

804
Ostrorog, *Count* Léon. The Angora reform. London, University of London Press, 1927. 99 p.
                                                  Law 28-18029

805
Osward, Maxim. Türkei, pforte des Orients. München, H. Aigner, 1964. 171 p.   DR429.074

806
Ottin, Merry. Comment peut-on être Turc. Paris, La Palatine, 1961. 206 p.   DR429.O8

807
Our treaty with Turkey. Advocate of peace, v. 88, April 1926: 247-250.   JX1901.W7, v. 88

808
Pace, Biagio. Della pianura di Adalia alle valle del Meandro; impressioni di viaggio. Milano, Casa Editrice Mondadori, 1927. 310 p.

809
Page, Kirby. Turkey in transition. World tomorrow, v. 12, Dec. 1929: 498-501.   HN51.W6, v. 12

810
Paillarès, Michel. Le Kémalisme devant les alliés. Paris, Edition du Bosphore, 1922. 494 p. DR589.P3

811
Pallis, Alexander A. The end of the Greco-Turkish feud. Contemporary review, v. 138, Oct. 1930: 615-620.   AP4.C7, v, 138

812
Pallis, Alexander A. Greece's Anatolian venture and after; a survey of the diplomatic and political aspects of the Greek expedition to Asia Minor (1915-1922). London, Methuen, 1937. 239 p.   DF833.P3

813
Pallis, Alexander A. The language reform in Turkey. *In* Royal Central Asian Society. Journal, v. 25, July 1938: 439-445.   DS1.R6, v. 25

814
Pallis, Alexander A. Population of Turkey in 1935. *In* Royal Geographical Society. Journal, v. 91, May 1938: 439-445.   G7.R91, v. 91

815
Palmer, Julian. Turkish politics: persons and parties. Nineteenth century and after, v. 108, Nov. 1930: 591-599.   AP4.N7, v. 108

816
Paloncy, Evžen. Turecko. Praha, Státní nakl. politické literatury, 1961. 113 p.   DR418.P27

817
Paneth, Philip. Turkey at the crossroads, a pictorial record. London, Alliance press, 1943. 80 p.   DR441.P3

818
Paneth, Philip. Turkey; decadence and rebirth. London, Alliance Press, 1943. 149 p.   DR577.P3

819
Papouktchieva, Maria. La politique de la Russie à l'égard des détroits. Genève, Impr. Grivet, 1944 188 p.   JX1393.S8P34

820
Parker, John. Turkey's international relations. Political quarterly, v. 15, April 1944: 148-158.   JAS.P72, v. 15

821
Parker, John *and* Charles Smith. Modern Turkey. London, G. Routledge, 1940. 259 p.   DR418.P3

822
Parker, Lockie. Green Bursa. Asia, v. 34, Dec. 1934: 746-750.   HF3119.A5, v. 34

823
Parker, Lockie. Women in new Turkey. Asia, v. 34, June 1934: 356-361.   HF3119.A5, v. 34

824
Pasvolski, Leo. Freedom of the Straits (Bosporus and Dardanelles); the emptiest of phrases. Advocate of peace, v. 85, Aug. 1923: 293-297.   JX1901.W7, v. 85

825
Paton, William, *and* M. M. Underhill. Ten years in Turkey. International review of missions, v. 21, Apr. 1932: 169-177.   BV2351.I6, v. 21

826
Patrick, Mary M. A Bosporus adventure; Istanbul (Constantinople) woman's college, 1871-1924. Stanford Calif., Stanford University Press, 1934. 284 p.   LF5323.C7P3

827
Patrick, Mary M. Social phases of the Turkish renaissance. New Orient, v. 3, July 1926: 25-28.   DS501.N6, v. 3

828
Patrick, Mary M. Under five sultans. New York, Century, 1929. 357 p.   DR568.8.P3A3

829

Patterson, Harriet L. Travelling through Turkey; an excursion into history and religion. Valley Forge, Judson Press, 1969. 191 p.   DR429.P35

830

Pavlova, Nelia. Au pays du Ghazi. Paris, Editions de la Revue Mondiale, 1930. 226 p.

831

Pavlovich, Mikh. Kemalistskoe dvizhenie v Turt͡sii. Krasnai͡a nov́, no. 1, ii͡un 1921: 218-228.
          AP50.K73, no. 1

832

Pech, Edgar. Les alliés et la Turquie. Paris, Les Presses Universitaires de France, 1925. 267 p.
          DR589.P4

833

Peffer, Nathaniel. Hands off in Turkey. Asia, v. 24, April 1924: 267-271.   HF3119.A5, v. 24

834

Peffer, Nathaniel. Turkey for the Turks. Asia, v. 24, Mar. 1924: 193-196.   HF3119.A5, v. 24

835

Peffer, Nathaniel. The Turkish republic. Asia, v. 24, Jan. 1924: 42-45, 76.   HF3119.A5, v. 24

-836

Peker, Recep. Volks und Staatswerdung Ausenpolitik. Europäische revue, v. 12, Juni 1936: 442-448.
          AP30.E8, v. 12

837

Pellegrineschi, Angelo V. La rivoluzione Kemalista e la nuova Turchia. Esercito e nazione, v. 6, dic. 1931: 1097-1103.   U4.N38, v. 6

838

Pereira, Michael. Mountains and a shore; a journey through Southern Turkey. London, Bles, 1966. 224 p.   DR429.P4

839

Pernot, Maurice. L'inquiétude de l'Orient; la reforme Turque. Revue des deux mondes, v. 39, 1 mai 1927: 75-105.   AP20.R3, v. 39

840

Pernot, Maurice. La nouvelle Turquie I: du Sultanat a la République. Revue des deux mondes, v. 19, 15 jan. 1924: 288-322.   AP20.R3, v. 19

841

Pernot, Maurice. La nouvelle Turquie II: l'ésprit et les tendances du nouveau régime. Revue des deux mondes, v. 19, 1 fév. 1924: 626-660.   AP20.R3, v. 19

842

Pernot, Maurice. La nouvelle Turquie III: le gouvernement d'Angora et les activités etrangères. Revue des deux mondes, v. 20, 1 mars 1924: 131-167.   AP20.R3, v. 20

843

Pernot, Maurice. La question Turque I: Constantinople sous le contrôle interallié. Revue des deux mondes, v. 7, 15 jan. 1922: 276-314.   AP20.R3, v. 7

844

Pernot, Maurice. La question Turque II: Angora; les Turcs entre l'Occident et l'Orient. Revue des deux mondes, v. 7, 1 fév. 1922: 549-579.   AP20.R3, v. 7

845

Pernot, Maurice. La question Turque III: les Turcs et l'Islam. Revue des deux mondes, v. 8, 1 mars 1922: 181-214.   AP20.R3, v. 8

846

Pernot, Maurice. La question Turque IV: les minorités non-Musulmanes et Turquie. Revue des deux mondes, v. 8, 15 avril 1922: 897-925.   AP20.R3, v. 8

847

Pernot, Maurice. La question Turque V: la Turquie et les puissances. Revue des deux mondes, v. 9, 15 mai 1922: 365-397.   AP20.R3, v. 9

848

Pernot, Maurice. La question Turque. Paris, B. Grasset, 1923. 332 p.   D463.P4

849

Pernot, Maurice. La réforme Kémaliste après Kemal Ataturk. L'Europe nouvelle, v. 21, 19 nov. 1938: 1255.   AP20.E88, v. 21

850

Peters, Richard F. Geschichte der Türken. Stuttgart, W. Kohlhammner Verlag, 1961. 223 p.

851
Peters, Richard F. Von der alten und neuen Türkei; gesammelte Aufsätze, 1. Folge. Ankara, Berkalp Kitabevi, 1944. 126 p.   DR441.P48

852
Phelan, Nancy (Creagh). Welcome the wayfarer; a traveller in modern Turkey. New York, St. Martin's Press, 1965. 243 p.   DR429.P45

853
Pillement, Georges. La Turquie inconnue; itinéraires archéologiques illustrés de 64 photographies de l'auteur. Paris, A. Michel, 1970. 412 p.   DR416.P55

854
Pinon, René. Les accords Franco-Turc. Revue des deux mondes, v. 46, 1 août 1938: 713-719.
                              AP20.R3, v. 46

855
Pinon, René. L'évolution de la question des Détroits. L'Esprit international, v. 2, avril 1928: 184-203.
                              JC362.A1E8, v. 2

856
Pinon, René. La Turquie et le sandjak d'Alexandrette. Revue des deux mondes, v. 37, 1 fév. 1937: 719-720.   AP20.R3, v. 37

857
Pinson, Mark. Turkish revolution and reform (1919-1928) in Soviet historiography. Middle East journal. v. 17, Autumn 1963: 466-478. DS1.M5, v. 17

858
Pittard, Eugène. A travers l'Asie Mineure; le visage nouveau de la Turquie. Paris, Société d'Editions Géographiques, Maritimes et Coloniales, 1931. 312 p.   OU

859
Pittard, Eugène. Hommages à la memoire d'Atatürk. Istanbul, Maarif Matbaası, 1939. 175 p.
                              DR592.K4P5

860
Plan of Russia and Turkey to control the Straits. Literary digest, v. 75, Oct. 21, 1922: 17-19.
                              AP2.L58, v. 75

861
Plimpton, George A. The United States and Lausanne treaty. New Orient, v. 3, July 1926: 20-24.
                              DS501.N6, v. 3

862
The political and strategic importance of Turkey. Bulletin of international news, v. 16, Nov. 4, 1939: 1167-1175.   D410.B8, v. 16

863
Polyzoides, Adamantios Th. The Greek collapse in Asia Minor. Current history, v. 17, Oct. 1922: 32-36.
                              D410.C8, v. 17

864
Polyzoides, Adamantios Th. Turkey's anti-Entente policy. Current history, v. 17, Dec. 1922: 496-498.
                              D410.C8, v. 17

865
Poulakos, Demetrios. Hē synchronos Tourkia kolnonika kai oikonomika themata. Athēnai, 1957. 135 p.
                              DR590.P6

866
Powers, Frederick P. The Lausanne treaty. New Armenia, v. 17, Jan.-Feb, 1925: 3-4. DS161.N47, v. 17

867
Poznanska, Krystyna. Turcja stara i nowa. Warszawa, Ludowa Spoldzelnia Wydawnicza, 1970. 317 p.
                              DR440.P67

868
Pravec, Karel. Kemal Atatürk. Praha, Svoboda, 1967, 173 p.

869
Pravec, Karel. Turecko. Praha, Svoboda, 1966. 149 p.
                              DR418.P7

870
Prayer and mosque attendance in Turkey. Moslem world, v. 18, Oct. 1928: 392-398.   DS36.M7, v. 18

871
Price, Claire. Foreign policy of the new Turkey. Current history, v. 17, Feb. 1923: 765-768. D410.C8, v. 17

872
Price, Claire. Kemal Pasha. Current history, v. 17, Nov. 1922: 318-322.   D410.C8, v. 17

873

Price, Claire. Kemal Pasha—creator of a new Turkey.
Current history, v. 16, July 1922: 584-594.
D410.C8, v. 16

874

Price, Claire. Mustafa Kemal and the Americans.
Current history, v. 17, Oct. 1922: 116-125.
D410.C8, v. 17

875

Price, Claire. Mustafa Kemal and the Angora government. Current history, v. 16, Aug. 1922: 790-800.
D410.C8, v. 16

876

Price, Claire. Mustapha Kemal and the Christians.
Current history, v. 16, Sept. 1922: 985-993.
D410.C8, v. 16

877

Price, Claire. Mustafa Kemal and the Greek war.
Current history, v. 14, Aug. 1921: 754-761.
D410.C8, v. 14

878

Price, Claire. Mustapha Kemal Pasha, the man.
Fortnightly review, v. 118, July 1922: 119-127.
AP4.F7, v. 118

879

Price, Claire. The new Turkey. Fortnightly review,
v. 118, Nov. 1922: 711-717.
AP4.F7, v. 118

880

Price, Claire. The rebirth of Turkey. New York, T.
Seltzer, 1923. 234 p.
DR589.P7

881

Price, Claire. Turkey and the Caliphate. Fortnightly
review, v. 118, Dec. 1922: 945-950.
AP4.F7, v. 118

882

Price, Claire. The Turkish national government.
Fortnightly review, v. 118, Oct. 1922: 561-568.
AP4.F7, v. 118

883

Price, Morgan P. A history of Turkey, from empire to
republic. London, Allen & Unwin, 1956. 224 p.
DR440.P7

884

Primi, Gilberto. Sus à l'envahisseur; de l'occupation

à la·libération de Smyrne. Constantinople, Presse
du Soir, 1922. 60 p.

885

Prison reform in Turkey. Moslem world, v. 27, July
1937: 316-317.
DS36.M7, v. 27

886

Psyroukes, Nikos M. Hē Mikrasiatike katastrophe
(1918-1923). Athēnai, Anexartetos Dromos, 1964.
272 p.
D469.G8P7

887

Puaux, René. Les derniers jours de Smyrne. Paris,
Revue des Balkans, 1923. 46 p.
DS51.I9P8

888

Puaux, René. La mort de Smyrne. Paris, Soc. Génér.
d'Imp. et d'Édit., 1922. 32 p.
DS51.S7P83

889

Pyzhova, L. Vysshaiâ shkola v novoi Turîsii. Vysshaiâ shkola, no. 4, 1937: 105-108. LB2300.V9, no. 4

890

La question d'Alexandrette. L'Asie française, v. 38,
sept.-oct. 1938: 241-247.
JV1801.A85, v. 38

891

Raber, Oran. New light on the destruction of Smyrna. Current history, v. 18, May 1923: 312-318.
D410.C8, v. 18

892

Raditsa, Bogdan. Turkey: the revolution that knew
when to stop; changes in the last 20 years. Reporter,
v. 6, Jan. 1954: 22-25.
D839.R385, v. 6

893

Ramaer, J. C. Het nieuwe Turkije. Haagsch maandblad, v. 10, nov. 1928: 504-526.
AP15.H3, v. 10

894

Ramaer, J. C. Turkije's grootheid en verval. Haagsch
maandblad, v. 10, oct. 1928: 371-381. AP15.H3, v. 10

895

Rapp, William J. The end of the Turkish Caliphate.
Nation, v. 118, Apr. 23, 1924: 474-475.
AP2.N2, v. 118

896

Rapp, William J. Republicanism in new Turkey. Current history, v. 19, Mar. 1924: 1038-1039.

D410.C8, v. 19

897

Raquette, Carl-Gustaf. Turkiets omdaring; en politisk och ekonomisk-geografisk översikt. Svensk geografisk arsbok, v. 11, 1935: 58-97.   G25.S8, v. 11

898

Ravndal, Gabriel B. Turkey: a commercial and industrial handbook. Washington, Govt. print. off. 1926. 232 p.   HC405.R3

899

Rawlings, Hoyt. The light of Turkish Ankara. Asia, v. 32, Mar. 1932: 148-152, 199-200.   HF3119.A5, v. 32

900

Rawlinson, *Sir* Alfred. Adventures in the Near East, 1918-1922. New York, Dodd, Mead & Co., 1924. 353 p.   D566.R3

901

Raymond, Alexandre M. Une ville célèbre: Angora. Paris, Geuthner, 1924. 103 p.

902

Recent economic developments in Turkey. Bankers', insurance managers' and agents' magazine, v. 145 Apr. 1938: 606-612.   HG1503.B2, v. 145

903

Réchad, Nihad (Belger). L'accord Franco-Turc. L'action nationale, v. 17, 25 nov. 1921: 126-136.

AP20.A3, v. 17

904

Réchad, Nihad (Belger). Les Grecs à Smyrne. Paris, Imp. Kossuth, 1920. 64 p.

905

Reed, Cass A. Education in the Turkish republic. Open court, v. 49, Oct. 1935: 225-235.

AP2.0495, v. 49

906

Reed, Howard A. Revival of Islam in secular Turkey. Middle East journal, v. 8, Summer 1954: 267-282.

DS1.M5, v. 8

907

Reed, Howard A. Secularism and Islam in Turkish politics. Current history, v. 32, June 1957: 333-338.

D410.C8, v. 32

908

Reforma alfavita v Turtsii. Novyi vostok, no. 25, 1929: 249-257.   YUDIN JN18.N9, no. 25

Signed: S. S.

909

Regnault, *Gen.* Choses de Turquie. Revue mondiale, v. 174, 1 déc., 1926: 211-220.   AP20.R25, v. 174

910

Relations Italo-Turques. L'Asie française, v. 32, juin 1932: 196-200.   JV1801, v. 32

Signed: "H. F."

911

Report on economic conditions in Turkey. London, H. M. Stationary Office, 1932. 46 p.

912

Reventlov, Chr. Asiatiske tider og maend. Kóbenhavn, C. A. Reitzels forlag, 1932. 320 p.

913

Réville, Louis. La Turquie et la crise Européenne. Politique étrangère, v. 3, oct. 1938: 489-504.

JX3.P6, v. 3

914

Reynolds, J. H. The new orthography in Turkey. Geographical journal, v. 74, July 1929: 72-74.

G7.R91, v. 74

915

Rice, Talbot. Some impressions of modern Turkey. *In* Royal Central Asian Society. Journal, v. 18, April 1931: 194-206.   DS1.R6, v. 18

916

Riedel, Herbert. Leibesübungen und körperliche erziehung in dor osmanischen und kâmalistischen Türkei. Würzburg, Triltsch, 1942. 90 p.

GV7.K6 hoft 14

917

Riggs, Charles T. Always something new in Turkey. Missionary review of the world, v. 58, Sept. 1935: 401-402.   BV2350.M7, v. 58

918

Riggs, Charles T. Religion in Turkey today. Missionary review of the world, v. 61, July-Aug. 1938: 327-329.   BV2350.M7, v. 61

919
Riggs, Charles T. Turkey fifty years ago and now.
Missionary review of the world, v. 51, Jan. 1928:
13-20.   BT2350.M7, v. 51

920
Riggs, Charles T. Turkey today. World dominion,
4 Dec. 1925: 48-56.   BV2000.W6, v. 4

921
Riggs, Charles T. Turkey, the treaties and the mis-
sionaries. Missionary review of the world, v. 50,
May 1927: 343-348.   BV2350.M7, v. 50

922
Riggs, Ernest W. The new era in Turkey. World dominion, v. 2, Dec. 1923: 19-24.   BV2000.W6, v. 2

923
Riggs, H. H. The missionary situation in Turkey.
International review of missions, v. 27, Apr. 1938:
195-200.   BV2351.I6, v. 27

924
The rise of Kemal and his Turks. Literary digest,
v. 75, Oct. 7, 1922: 9-10.   AP2.L58, v. 75

925
Rivkin, Malcolm D. Area development for national
growth; the Turkish precedent. New York, Praeger, 1965. 228 p.   HC405.R5

926
Roberts, Thomas D. Area handbook for the Republic
of Turkey. Washington, U. S. Govt. Print. Off.,
1970. 438 p.   DR417.R54

927
Robinson, Richard D. The First Turkish Republic;
a case study in national development. Cambridge,
Harvard University Press, 1963. 367 p.
                                  DR590.R62

928
Robinson, Richard D. The lesson of Turkey. The
Middle East journal, v. 5, Autumn 1951: 424-438.
                                  DS1.M5, v. 5

929
Robinson, Richard D. Mosque and school in Turkey.
Moslem world, v. 51, Apr. 1961: 107-110; July
1961: 185-188.   DS36.M7, v. 51

930
Roccalta, Pierluigi di. Angora e Kemal Pascià; pro-
blemi politici ed economici della moderna Turchia. Roma, A. R. E., 1932. 234 p.

931
Roche, Maurice. Évolution de la question des Détroits: Bosphore et Dardanelles. Revue des sciences politiques, v. 56, juil. 1933: 429-448.
                                  H3.R35, v. 56

932
Roedenbeck, Georg. Das Turkische Reich-ein Bren-
npunkt politischen Geschehens. Berlin, Verlags-
anstalt Otto Stollberg, 1939. 100 p.   DR441.R6

933
Rössler, Fritz. Kemal Pascha. Berlin, R. Kittlers
Verlag, 1934. 122 p.

934
Rössler, Fritz. Welchen Weg geht die Türkei? Das
Aufbauwerk Atatürks während seiner fünfzehnjäh-
rigen Regierungstätigkeit und die Politik Anka-
ras nach dem Tode des Schöpfers der neuen Türkei. Dresden, Krueger & Horn, 1940. 142 p.
                                  DR589.R57

935
Röthlisberger, Marcel. Die Türkei; Reise durch ih-
re Geschichte. Bern, Kümmerly & Frey, 1959. 204 p.
                                  DR429.R6

936
Roger, Nöelle. En Asie-Mineure; la Turquie du Ghazi. Paris, Fasquelle Editeurs, 1930. 264 p.
                                  N.Y.P.L.

937
Roger, Noëlle. La Turquie de Kémal Ataturk: Ana-
dolou. Revue des deux mondes, v. 48, 1 déc. 1938:
601-623.   AP20.R3, v. 48

938
Rohrbach, Paul. Balkan-Türkei, eine schicksalszone
Europas. Hamburg, Hoffmann und Campe, 1940.
96 p.   DR37.R6

939
Ronart, Otto. L'industrialisation de la Turquie. Revue économique internationale, v. 30, déc. 1938:
515-532.   HB3.R5, v. 30

940
Ronart, Stephan. Die Türkei von heute. Amsterdam, Édition Pays et Peuples, Verlag de Steenuil, 1936. 267 p.   DR589.R6

941
Rondot, Pierre. La Turquie et les problèmes Méditerranéens. Politique étrangère, v. 4, août 1939: 536-551.   JX3.P6, v. 4

942
Ross, *Sir* E. Denison. Making of modern Turkey. *In* Royal Central Asian Society. Journal, v. 24, Apr. 1937: 217-233.   DS1.R6, v. 24

943
Ross, Irwin. From Atatürk to Gürsel; what went wrong in Turkey. New leader, v. 43, Dec. 1960: 14-18.   HX1.N37, v. 43

944
Ross, *Sir* E. Denison. The westernization of Turkey. Great Britain and east, v. 50, Mar. 17, 1938: 293-294.   D461.G8, v. 50

945
Rossi, Ettore. Atatürk; 1880-1938. Oriente moderno, v. 18, dic. 1938: 635-646.   D461.07, v. 18

946
Rossi, Ettore. Il decennale della republica turca. Oriente moderno, v. 13, nov. 1933: 541-557.   D461.07, v. 13

947
Rossi, Ettore. Il "Ghazi" Mustafà Kemal Pascià. Gerarchia, v. 9, mar. 1929: 297-304.   D410.G43, v. 9

948
Rossi, Ettore. La nuova Turchia. Roma, Edizioni Roma, 1939. 160 p.   DR589.R7

949
Rossi, Ettore. Il nuovo alfabeto Latino introdotto in Turchia. Oriente moderno, v. 9, genn. 1929: 32-48.   D461.07, v. 9

950
Rossi, Ettore. La questione dell'alfabeto per le lingue Turche. Oriente moderno, v. 7, giugno 1927: 295-310.   D461.07, v. 7

951
Rossi, Ettore. La riforma linguistica in Turchia. Oriente moderno, v. 15, genn. 1935: 45-57.   D461.07, v. 15

952
Roten, Iris. Vom Bosporus zum Euphrat; Türken und Türkei. Stuttgart, H. Goverts, 1965. 264 p.   DR429.R63

953
Roucek, Joseph S. The Turk and his politics. World affairs interpreter, v. 10, July 1939: 177-184.   AP2.W74825, v. 10

954
Rougier, Antoin. La question des Détroits et la convention de Lausanne. Revue générale de droit international public, v. 31, sept.-oct. 1924: 309-338.   JX3.R56, v. 31

955
Rouillon, Léon. Mon beau voyage; la Turquie et ses ennemies, jugés par un soldat français. Paris, Editions Les Gémeaux, 1923. 167 p.   N.Y.P.L.

956
Roux, Jean P. La Turquie; geographie, économie, histoire, civilization et culture. Paris, Payot, 1953. 192 p.   DR417.R6

957
Rozaliev, Iurii N. Klassy i klassovaia borba v Turt͡sii, burzhuazii͡a i proletariat. Moskva, Nauka, 1966. 165 p.   HC405.R59

958
Rozaliev, Iurii N. Osobennosti razvitii͡a kapitalizma v Turt͡sii, 1923-1960 gg. Moskva, Izd-Vo vostochnoi lit-ry, 1962. 354 p.   HC405.R6

959
Rühl, Philip, *ed.* Die Türkische Republik in Wirtschaft und Aufbau. Frankfurt a. Main, R. T. Hauser, 1925. 94 p.   HC405.R8

960
Russian-Turkish relations. Nation, v. 116, Jan. 24, 1923: 103-104.   AP2.N2, v. 116

961
Russian view of the republic Kemal built. Literary digest, v. 83, Nov. 8, 1924: 18-19.   AP2.L58, v. 83

962
Rustem, Alfred. Turkey taking her place among modern nations. Current history, v. 25, Feb. 1927: 669-675.   D410.C8, v. 25

963
Rustem, Alfred. Les victoires d'Angora. Revue de Genève, v. 5, déc. 1922: 771-786.   AP24.B44, v. 5

964
Rustow, Dankwart A. The army and the founding of the Turkish republic. World politics, v. 11, July 1959: 513-552.   D839.W57, v. 11

965
Rustow, Dankwart A. *comp.* Atatürk as founder of a state. *In his* Philosophers and kings; studies in leadership. New York, G. Braziller, 1970. p. 208-247.
                    HM141.R83

966
Rustow, Dankwart A. Atatürk's political leadership. *In* New York University Near Eastern Round Table, 1st. 1967-1968. New York, New York University Near East Center, 1969. p. 143-155.
                    DS252.4.N48

967
Rustow, Dankwart A. The development of parties in Turkey. *In* La Palombara, Joseph G. *ed.* Political parties and political development. Princeton, N. J., Princeton University Press, 1966. p. 107-133.
                    JF2051.P25

968
Rustow, Dankwart A. Foreign policy of the Turkish Republic; 1923-1939. *In* Macridis, Roy C. *ed.* Foreign policy in world politics. Englewood Cliffs, N. J., Prentice-Hall, 1962. p. 295-322.
                    JX1391.M32

969
Rustow, Dankwart A. Middle Eastern political systems. Englewood Cliffs, N. J., Prentice-Hall, 1971. 114 p.   JF51.R84

970
Rustow, Dankwart A. Politics and Islam in Turkey. *In* Harvard University. Summer School of Arts and Sciences and of Education. Islam and the West; proceedings of the Harvard Summer School conference on the Middle East, July 25-27, 1955. Gravenhage, Mouton, 1957. p. 69-107.   DS38.H35

971
Rustow, Dankwart A. Politics and westernization in the Near East. Princeton, N. J., Center of International Studies, Princeton University, 1956. 38 p.
                    DS63.R8

972
Rustow, Dankwart A. Turkey. *In* Near East Conference. 18th. Princeton, N. J., 1966. Political modernization in the Near East and North Africa; papers. Princeton, N. J., 1966. p. 97-109.   DS63.N4

973
Rustow, Dankwart A. Turkey: the tradition of modernity. *In* Pye, Lucian, *and* Sidney Verba, *eds.* Political culture and political development. Princeton, N. J., Princeton University Press, 1965. p. 171-198.
                    JF2011.P9

974
Rydh, Hanna. Det omvandlade Turkiet. Jorden runt, v. 20, jan. 1948: 1-17.   G149.J54, v. 20

975
Rygaard, Olaf A. Mellem tyrker og kurder; en dansk ingeniors oplevelser i Lilleasien. Kobenhavn, Gyldendal, 1935. 176 p.   DR428.R9

976
Rynd, Francis F. Turkish racial theories. *In* Royal Central Asian Society. Journal, v. 21, July 4, 1934: 476-487.   DS1.R6, v. 21

977
Sablier, Édouard. D'Ataturk à la IIe République Turque. Revue de Paris, v. 68, Nov. 1961: 42-52.
                    AP20.R27, v. 68

978
Sachar, Howard M. The emergence of the Middle East: 1914-1924. New York, Knopf, 1969. 518 p.
                    DS62.9.S23

979
Sadak, Necmeddin. Turkey faces the Soviets. Foreign affairs, v. 27, April 1949: 449-461.   D410.F6, v. 27

980
Sagay. S. Reşat. La nouvelle Turquie et la communauté internationale; étude d'histoire, de diplo-

matie et de droit international. Strasbourg, Librairie uiversitaire d'Alsace, 1936. 242 p.

JX1568.S2

981

Šahinović-Ekremov, Munir. Turska, danas i sjutra; prosjek kroz život jedne države. Sarajevo, Muslimanska Svijest, 1939. 192 p.

982

Sakazova, Vera. La femme Turque. Les Balkans, v. 2, fév.-mars 1932: 318-319. DR1.B35, v. 2

983

Samylovskiĭ, I. V. Turt͡sii͡a-votchina Uoll-strita. Moskva, Gos. izd-vo polit. lit-ry, 1952. 78 p.

DR578.S35

984

Sanguineti, Vittorio. La politica industriale della Turchia. Rivista Italiana di scienze economiche, v. 11, genn. 1939: 62-81. HB7.R5, v. 11

985

Sarajilić, Šemsudin. Nova Turska. Sarajevo, Hrvatska tiskara, 1930. 142 p. DR589.S2

986

Sargsyan, Ervand K. Velikai͡a Oktii͡abr'skai͡a revoli͡ut͡sii͡a i nat͡sional'no-osvoboditel'nai͡a bor'ba v Turt͡sii (1918-1922). Erevan, Izd-vo AH Armii͡anskoi SSR, 1958. 79 p. DR589.S22

987

Saunders, R. M. The new Turkey: an account of the changes which have brought into existence the modern Turkish republic and the significance of Turkey today. Current affairs, v. 3, Sept. 15, 1953: 4-30. D839.C863, v. 3

988

Savadjian, Léon. La politique extérieure de la Turquie et le probleme de la paix balkanique. L'Europe nouvelle, v. 16, déc. 16, 1933: 1206-1209.

AP20.E88, v. 16

989

Savant, Jean. La Turquie d'aujourd'hui. Revue des deux mondes, v. 70, July 1, 1942: 76-85.

AP20.R3, v. 70

990

Schlesinger, Nathan. Le nouveau régime des Détroits. Paris, Jouve, 1926. 119 p.

MH
N.Y.P.L.

991

Schlicklin, Jean. Angora; l'aube de la Turquie nouvelle (1919-1922). Paris, Berger-Levrault, 1922. 349 p.
DR589.S3

992

Schlicklin, Jean. Les opérations militaires. L'Europe nouvelle, v. 5, 16 sept. 1922: 1162-1163.

AP20.E88, v. 5

993

Schlicklin, Jean. Opinions Turques. Orient et occident, v. 5, 15 mai 1923: 5-14. DS.045, v. 5

994

Schmidt-Dumont, Franz F. Das Türkische Verkehrswesen. Europäische revue, v. 12, Juni 1936: 490-497.

AP30.E8, v. 12

995

Schmidt, Nathaniel. The peace of Lausanne. American review, v. 2, Jan. 1924: 55-58. AP2.A43, v. 2

996

Schopen, Edmund. Die neue Türkei. Leipzig, Goldmann, 1938. 149 p. DR441.S3

997

Schreiner, George A. The Turkish Straits under international control. Current history, v. 21, Oct. 1924: 65-74. D410.C8, v. 21

998

Scipio, Lynn A. My thirty years in Turkey. Rindge, N. H., R. R. Smith, 1955. 364 p. TA140.S35A3

999

Scrapping the Treaty of Sèvres. Literary digest, v. 70, Aug. 27, 1921: 14-15. AP2.L58, v. 70

1000

Seifullin, Lidiia N. V strane ukhodiashchego Islama, poezdka v Turt͡sii͡u. Leningrad, Gosizdat, 1925. 145 p.

1001

Sforza, Carlo, *conte.* How we lost the war with Turkey. Contemporary review, v. 132, Nov. 1927: 583-589. AP4.C7, v. 132

1002
Sforza, Carlo, *conte*. Mustafa Kemal. *In his* Makers of modern Europe. Indianapolis, Bobbs-Merill, 1930. p. 354-373. D412.S4

1003
Sforza, Carlo, *conte*. The Turkish dictatorship, *In his* European dictatorships. New York, Brentano's, 1931. p. 195-209. D720.S3

1004
Shah, Ikbal A. Kamal: maker of modern Turkey. London, H. Joseph, 1934. 297 p. DR592.K4S45

1005
Shah, Ikbal A. Mustapha Kamal. *In his* The controlling minds of Asia. London, Jenkins, 1937. p. 11-46. DS32.S5

1006
Shamsutdinov, A. M. Natsionalno-osvoboditelnaia borba v Turtsii, 1918-1923. Moskva, Nauka, 1966. 358 p. DR589.S47

1007
Shamsutdinov, A. M. Turetskaia Respublika; kratkii ocherk istorii, 1923-1961. Moskva, Izd-vo vostochno—lit-ry, 1962. 94 p. DR590.S5

1008
Shantić, Krsta S. Le miracle turc. Paris, La Renaissance Moderne, 1929. 184 p.

1009
Shepstone, H. J. In Turkey's new capital. Sphere, v. 144, Feb. 22, 1936: 330-331. AP4.S73, v. 144

1010
Sheridan, *Mrs.* Clare C. (Frewen). A Turkish kaleidoscope. London, Duckworth, 1926. 223 p. DR428.S5

1011
Sherrill, Charles H. Kamal-Roosevelt-Mussolini. Bologna, N. Zanichelli, 1936. 307 p. D412.6.S53

1012
Sherrill, Charles H. My interviews with the Gazi. Asia, v. 34, Mar. 1934: 140-143. HF3119.A5, v. 34

1013
Sherrill, Charles H. Venizelos faces East. Review of reviews, v. 83, June 1931: 64-66. AP2.R4, v. 83

1014
Sherrill, Charles H. A year's embassy to Mustafa Kemal. New York, C. Scribner's Sons, 1934. 277 p. DR592.K4S5

1015
Shotwell, James T., *and* Francis Deak. Turkey at the straits. New York, MacMillan, 1940. 196 p. DR741.B7S5

1016
Simonds, Frank H. Greek versus Turk; a new phase of the Eastern question. American review of reviews, v. 62, Aug. 1920: 159-168. AP2.R4, v. 62

1017
Simonds, Frank H. The return of the Turk. American review of reviews, v. 66, Oct. 1922: 482-491. AP2.R4, v. 66

1018
Simskii, L. Shkola v Turtsii. Narodnyi uchitel, no. 1, 1934: 111-114. Unclass. Cyr. N-9 CSt-H

1019
Singer, Kurt. Europas diktatorer. Stockholm, A. Holmströms Förlag, 1936. 112 p. D412.6.S53

1020
Skinner, Robert P. The new Turkey. American foreign service journal, v. 12, Apr. 1935: 189-191, 242. JX1.A53, v. 12

1021
Slater, Mary. The golden link, a novel based on the life of Mustafa Kemal. New York, Exposition Press, 1962. 425 p. PZ4.S63114

1022
Sleeswijk, J. G. Turkije, ouden nieuw. Haagsch maandblad, v. 28, sept. 1937: 289-295. AP15.H3, v. 28

1023
Smirnov, Viacheslav P. Turtsiia; zkonomika i vneshniaia torgovlia. Moskva, Vneshtorgizdat, 1956. 95 p. HC405.S53

1024

Smith, Elaine D. Turkey; origins of the Kemalist movement and the government of the Grand National Assembly, 1919-1923. Washington, 1959. 175 p.   DR589.S55

1025

Smogorzewski, K. M. New Turkey's first twenty-five years. Contemporary review, v. 174, Dec. 1948: 326-330.   AP2.C698, v. 174

1026

Sokolnicki, Michal. The Turkish Straits. Beirut, American Press. 1950. 44 p.   D468.S6

1027

Sokoľskiĭ, N. Ocherki sovremennoĭ Turt͡sii. Tiflis, Izd. Zakkraĭkoma RKP, 1923. 207 p.

1028

Some changes in Turkish thought. International review of missions, v. 15, Apr. 1926: 177-192.   BV2351.I6, v. 15

1029

The sort of man Mustafa Kemal is. Literary digest, v. 75, Oct. 14, 1922: 50-53.   AP2.L58, v. 75

1030

The Soviet, Turkey and the Kurds. World dominion, v. 8. Oct. 1930: 356.   BV2000.W6, v. 8

1031

Spector, Ivar. The Soviet-Turkish rapprochement, 1917-25. *In his* The Soviet Union and the Muslim world, 1917-1958. Seattle, University of Washington Press, 1956. p. 63-83.   DS63.2.R9S65

1032

Spencer, Robert F. Culture process and intellectual current: Durkheim and Atatürk. American anthropologist, v. 60, Aug. 1958: 640-657.   GN1.A5, v. 60

1033

Spencer, William. The land and people of Turkey. Philadelphia, Lippincott, 1958. 128 p.   DR428.S7

1034

Spender, J. A. Turkey today. International affairs, v. 6, Mar. 1927: 105-111.   JX1.I53, v. 6

1035

Speranskiĭ, A. F. Turet͡skiĭ vopros na mezhdunarodnykh konferentsii͡akh posle mirovoĭ voĭny. Novyi vostok, no. 2, 1922: 126-146.   YUDIN JN18.N9, no. 2

1036

Sperco, Willy. Moustapha Kemal Ataturk, 1882-1938. Paris, Nouvelles Éditions Latines, 1958. 204 p.   DR592.K4S6

1037

Sperco, Willy. Turcs d'hier et d'aujourd'hui, Paris, Nouvelles Éditions Latines, 1961. 187 p.   DR432.S66

1038

Spies, Otto. Modern Turkey and Islam. Islamic review, v. 22, Aug. 1934: 272-287.   BP1.I7, v. 22

1039

Sprengling, Martin. Modern Turkey: a scion, not a stage of Ottoman Turkey. Open court, v. 46, May 1932: 281-290.   AP2.O495, v. 46

1040

Sproule, James A. Who burned Smyrna? Islamic review, v. 11, Aug. 1923: 280-284.   BP1.I7, v. 11

1041

Spyridonos, Georgios L. Polemos Kai eleutheriai e Mikrasiatike ektratia hopos ten eida. Athēnai, 1957. 282 p.   DF845.S6

1042

Stanley, Brian. Turkish schools; seen through the eyes of an English visitor. School and society, v. 40, Dec. 15, 1934: 814-819.   L11.S36, v. 40

1043

Stephanove, C. Why France is helping the Turks. Current history, v. 16, July 1922: 655-657.   D410.C8, v. 16

1044

Stevens, Elbert C. The Turkish republic, 1925. Current history, v. 21, Mar. 1925: 900-906.   D410.C8, v. 21

1045

Stewart, Desmond S. Turkey. New York, Time-Life Books, 1969. 160 p.   DR429.S7

1046
Stirling, Paul. Religious change in republican Turkey. Middle East journal, v. 12, Autumn 1958: 395-408.   DS1.M5, v. 12

1047
Stoddard, Lothrop. Mustapha Kemal: Incarnation of new Turkey. New Orient, v. 2, June 1925: 33-41.
                                         DS501.N6, v. 2

1048
Stolte, J. G. Turkije. Baarn, Het Wereldvenster, 1969. 224 p.   DR429.S74

1049
Stotz, Carl L. Coastal lands of the sea of Marmara. Journal of geography, v. 32, Nov. 1933: 305-315.
                                         G1.J87, v. 32

1050
Stotz, Carl L. The human geography of the Dardanelles. Journal of geography, v. 34, May 1935: 173-186.   G1.J87, v. 34

1051
Stotz, Carl L. Turkish statistical material. Geographical review, v. 28, Jan. 1938: 154.   G1.G35, v. 28

1052
Streit, Gorgios. Der Lausanner Vertrag und der Griechisch-Türkische Bevölkerungsaustausch. Berlin, Georg Stilke, 1929. 71 p.   JX77.K55

1053
Strupp, Karl. Die Beziehungen zwischen Griechenland und der Türkei von 1820-1930. Breslau, J. U. Kern's verlag, 1932. 158 p.

1054
Strupp, Karl. Der Vertrag von Lausanne. Berlin, Emil Roth, 1932. 67 p.   D648.L35

1055
Stuart, James. The failure of the Lausanne conference. Fortnightly review, v. 120, Oct. 1923: 574-581.
                                         AP4.F7, v. 120

1056
Suche, Joachim. Der Meerengenvertrag von Montreux vom 20. Juli 1936 und seine Torgeschite (seit 1918). München, Duncker, 1936. 73 p.
                                         D462-1936 j

1057
Süreyya, Şevket (Aydemir). Die soziale Bedeutung der Türkischen Revolution. Europäische revue, v. 12, Juni 1936: 500-506.   AP30.E8, v. 12

1058
Susa, Nasim. The capitulatory régime of Turkey, its history, origin and nature. Baltimore, Johns Hopkins Press, 1933. 378 p.   JX1568.S8

1059
Svara, Maksim. Gazi Mustafa Kemal Paša; njegov život i djela. Sarajevo, Islamska Dionieka Stamperija, 1931. 111 p.

1060
Sverchevskaiâ, A. K. Bibliografiiâ Turtsii. 1917-1958. Moskva, Izd-vo vostochnoĭ, 1959. 189 p.   Z2846.S9

1061
Svetovski, Mihailoviç. Ataturkova Turska. Beograd, Balkanskog Insituta, 1938. 250 p.

1062
Szirmai, Rezsö. Mussolini, Kemál, Sztalin és a többiek. Budapest, Viktoria Kiadas, 1935. 226 p.

1063
Tachau, Frank. Language and politics: Turkish language reform. Review of politics, v. 26, Apr. 1964: 191-204.   JA1.R4, v. 26

1064
Taeschner, Franz G., and Gotthard Jäschke. Aus der Geschiste des islamischen Orients. Tübingen, Mohr, 1949. 40 p.   DS36.4.T3

1065
Taillardat, F. L'activité économique de la Turquie. L'Asie française, v. 37, déc. 1937: 300-303.
                                         JV1801.A85, v. 37

1066
Taillardat, F. Ataturk. L'Asie française, v. 39, jan. 1939: 6-13.   JV1801.A85, v. 39

1067
Taillardat, F. L'influence soviétique dans l'économie turque. L'Asie française, v. 34, sept.-oct. 1934: 246-249.   JV1801.A85, v. 34

1068
Taillardat, F. La nouvelle convention des Détroits.

L'Asie française, v. 36, juil./août 1936: 201-211.
JV1801.A85, v. 36

1069
Taillardat, F. Quelques aspects de la politique exterieure turque. L'Asie française, v. 38, juil.-août 1938: 202-210.　　JV1801.A85, v. 38

1070
Taillardat, F. La remilitarisation des Détroits. L'Asie française, v. 36, mai 1936: 139-143.
JV1801.A85, v. 36

1071
Talat, A. La constitution turque du 20 avril, 1924. Chambéry, Imprimerie Réunies, 1935. 131 p.
JN9715.T3

1072
Tanca, Semih. Les resources minéralogiques de la Turquie et son régime minier. Toul, Imprimerie touloise, 1937. 251 p.　　TN111.T3

1073
Tarle, E. V. Angliiâ i Turt͡siiâ. Annaly, no. 3, 1923: 21-71.　　D1.A5, no. 3

1074
Telegramma V. I. Lenina M. Kemaliû. Kommunist, no. 15, okt. 1957: 13-14.　　HX8.K56, no. 15

1075
Telford, J. Turkish revival. London quarterly review, v. 153, Apr. 1930: 253-259.　　AP4.L53, v. 153

1076
Ténékidès, C. G. Le statut des minorités et l'échange obligatoire des populations Gréco-Turques. Revue générale de droit international public, v. 31, jan.-avril 1924: 72-88.　　JX3.R56, v. 31

1077
Thayer, Lucius E. Capitulations of the Ottoman empire and the question of their abrogation as it affects the United States. American journal of international law, v. 17, Apr. 1923: 207-233.
JX1.A6, v. 17

1078
Theodore, Demetrios E. The sacrificials; part of an autobiography depicting the life of minorities in a war torn country. Boston, Branden Press, 1970. 127 p.　　DR589.T46

1079
Thomas, Lewis V. Turkish Islam. Moslem world, v. 44, July-Oct. 1954: 181-185.　　DS36.M7, v. 44

1080
Thomas, Lewis V., *and* Richard N. Frye. The United States and Turkey and Iran. Cambridge, Harvard University Press, 1951. 291 p.　　E183.T8T5

1081
Thornburg, Max W., Graham Spry *and* George Soule. Turkey, an economic appraisal. New York, Twentieth Century Fund, 1949. 324 p.　HC405.T46

1082
The Times, London, Turkish number. London, 1938.
DR589.T5

1083
Tobin, Chester M. Turkey, key to the East. New York, G. P. Putnam's sons, 1944. 170 p.　DR441.T6

1084
Todorov, Nikolaĭ. Natsionalno-osvoboditelnoto dvizhenie v Turt͡siia sled purvata svetovna voina i utvurzhdavaneto na Kemalizma. Istoricheski pregled, v. 8, no. 2, 1951: 175-198.　　DR51.B883, v.8

1085
Todorov, Nikolaĭ. Velezhit deets na Turskiia narod. (Mustafa Kemal Atatiurk). Istoricheski pregled, v. 20, no. 1, 1964: 3-11.　　DR51.B883, v. 20

1086
Tomič, Zoran. Kamal Ataturk, tvorac nove Turske. Beograd, Št. Planeta, 1939. 294 p.

1087
Tomlin, Eric W. Turkey: the modern miracle. London, Watts, 1940. 46 p.　　DR589.T58

1088
Tongas, Gérard. Atatürk et le vrai visage de la Turquie moderne. Paris, P. Geuthner, 1937. 99 p.　　DR589.T6

1089
Tongas, Gérard. La Turquie, centre de gravité des Balkans et du Proche-Orient. Paris, P. Geuthner, 1939. 276 p.　　DR590.T6

1090

Topalović, Živko. Turska. Beograd, Izdavačka knji-
žarnica kona, 1932. 87 p.   DR428.T6

1091

Toscano, Mario. La conferanza di Montreux e la nuova convenzione degli stretti. Milano, Gontra-
no Martucci editore, 1938. 228 p.   MH

1092

Tosević, Dimitrije J. Mustafa Kemal Atatürk; moder-
ni Turecko Mustafe Kemala Ataturka. Praha, Praha Nakladatelstvi Orbus, 1935. 236 p.

1093

Tosti, Amedeo. Kemal Atatürk soldato e statista
della nuova Turchia. Rassegna di cultura militare,
v. 17, apr. 1939: 350-359.   U4.R25, v. 17

1094

Toto, Ismet. Skicë jeteshkrimi Gazi Kemal Atatürk.
Tiranë, Shtypshkroja, 1935. 195 p.

1095

Townshend, *Sir* Charles. Great Britain and the Turks.
Asia, v. 22, Dec. 1922: 949-953.   HF3119.A5, v. 22

1096

Toynbee, Arnold J. Angora, Cinderella—metropolis
of Turkey. Asia, v. 23, Sept. 1923: 714-718, 764-765.
                                       HF3119.A5, v. 23

1097

Toynbee, Arnold J. The dénouement in the Near
East. Contemporary review, v. 122, Oct. 1922:
409-418.   AP4.C7, v. 122

1098

Toynbee, Arnold J. East after Lausanne. Foreign
affairs, v. 2, Sept. 15, 1923: 84-99.   D410.F6, v. 2

1099

Toynbee, Arnold J. Meeting the Turk half way. Asia,
v. 23, Aug. 1923: 576-581.   HF3119.A5, v. 23

1100

Toynbee, Arnold J. Mustafa Kemal. *In* Men of tur-
moil; biographies by leading authorities of the
dominating personalities of our day. Freeport,
N. Y., Books for Libraries Press, 1969. p. 174-183.
                                             D412.G7

1101

Toynbee, Arnold J. New economic aims in Turkey.

Asia, v. 23, Sept. 1923: 660-663, 686-687.
                                       HF3119.A5, v. 23

1102

Toynbee, Arnold J. Turkey and China. Asia, v. 30,
June 1930: 420-425, 448-451.   HF3119.A5, v. 30

1103

Toynbee, Arnold J. Turkey revisited. Contemporary
review, v. 136, Oct. 1929: 458-464.   AP4.C7, v. 136

1104

Toynbee, Arnold J. The Turkish state of mind. Atlantic monthly, v. 136, Oct. 1925: 548-560.
                                         AP2.A8, v. 136

1105

Toynbee, Arnold J. The Western question in Greece
and Turkey; a study in the contact of civilisations.
London, Constable, 1923. 408 p.   D465.T6

1106

Toynbee, Arnold J., *and* Kenneth P. Kirkwood.
Turkey. New York, C. Scribner's, 1927. 329 p.
                                             DR476.T7

1107

Toynbee, Rosalind. Turkish woman of today. Forum,
v. 80, Sept. 1928: 412-420.   AP2.F8, v. 80

1108

Trask, Roger R. Joseph C. Grew and Turco-American
rapprochement, 1927-1932. *In* Brown, Sydney D.
Studies on Asia, v. 8, 1967. Lincoln, University of
Nebraska Press, 1967. p. 139-170.   DS2.S8

1109

Trask, Roger R. The United States and Turkish
nationalism: investments and technical aid during
the Atatürk era. Business history review, v. 38,
Spring 1964: 58-77.   HF5001.B8262, v. 38

1110

Trask, Roger R. The United States response to Turkish nationalism and reform, 1914-1939. Minnea-
polis, University of Minnesota Press, 1971. 280 p.
                                           E183.8.T8T7

1111

Trask, Roger R. "Unnamed Christianity" during the
Atatürk era. Moslem world, v. 55, Jan. 1955: 66-76;
Apr. 1955: 101-111.   DS36.M7, v. 55

1112

Treaty of peace with Turkey, and other Instruments signed at Lausanne on July 24, 1923, together with agreements between Greece and Turkey signed on 30th January 1923, and subsidiary documents forming part of the Turkish Peace Settlement. Melbourne, A. J. Mullet, 1924. 48 p.   D462 1923 b

1113

Treaty with Turkey: the full text of the treaty signed at Moscow on March 16 by the governments of Russia and Turkey. Soviet Russia, v. 5, Sept. 1921: 109-111.   DK266.A2S7, v. 5

1114

Trikoupēs, Nikolaos. Anamnēseis epeisodiōn kai gegonotōn ek tōn polemōn mas. Athēnai, Edkolikon Tmēma Institonton Lampadia, 1952. 141 p.   DR765.T7

1115

Trobayre, Jean. Ce qu'il faut connaitre des Turcs et de leur histoire. Paris, Boivin, 1935. 160 p.

1116

Tröbst, Hans. Soldatenblut vom Baltikum zu Kemal Pascha. Leipzig, K. F. Koehler, 1925. 330 p.
N.Y.P.L.
CSt-H

1117

Tsamados, M. Greek defeat in Turkey an allied disaster. Current history, v. 18, May 1923: 218-222.   D410.C8, v. 18

1118

Türk Tarih Kurumu. Histoire de la République turque. İstanbul, Devlet Basımevi, 1935. 372 p.   DR589.T83

1119

Türkiye cumhuriyet halk partisi. Turquie 1938; quinzième anniversaire de la proclamation de la République turque (29 octobre 1938). Istanbul, Imprimerie Djumhuriet, 1938. 82 p.   DR589.T9T8

1120

Tütsch, H. E. Turkey and the West; the bases of present policy. Swiss review of world affairs, v. 1, Jan. 1, 1951: 13-15.   D839.S9, v. 1

1121

Turcot, Henri. External trade of Turkey. In Canada.

Dept. of Trade and Commerce. Commercial intelligence journal, v. 44, Mar. 7, 1931: 299-302.
HF129.A27, v. 44

1122

Turcot, Henri. External trade of Turkey in 1936. In Canada. Dept. of Trade and Commerce. Commercial intelligence journal, v. 56, May 22, 1937: 907-908.   HF129.A27, v. 56

1123

Turcot, Henri. Turkey as a market. In Canada. Dept. of Trade and Commerce. Commercial intelligence journal, v. 60, Apr. 22, 1939: 586-595.
HF129.A27, v. 60

1124

Turcot, Henri. Turkey in 1935. In Canada. Dept. of Trade and Commerce. Commercial intelligence journal, v. 55, Nov. 14, 1936: 921-924.
HF129.A27, v. 55

1125

Turcot, Henri. Turkey in 1937. In Canada. Dept. of Trade and Commerce. Commercial intelligence journal, v. 59, July 2, 1938: 30-31.   HF129.A27, v. 59

1126

The Turk on top again. Outlook v. 126, Dec. 15, 1920: 670-671.   AP2.08, v. 126

1127

Turkey and the Allies. Economist, v. 95, Sept. 16, 1922: 462.   HG11.E2, v. 95

1128

Turkey and America; editorial symposium. Living age, v. 332, Mar. 15, 1927: 491-493.   AP2.L65, v. 332

1129

Turkey. Basın-Yayın ve Turizm Vekâleti. Turkey on the way of industrialization. Ankara, 1937. 48 p.
HC405.A4

1130

Turkey. Büyük Millet Meclisi. (Proces-verbaux des travaux parlementaires) Angora, 1920—1st legislature, 1920-1923; 6th legislature, 2d sess., 1941. Compte rendu des debats de la Grande assemblée nationale.   J461.H3

1131

Turkey and the caliphs. Youth's companion, v. 98, Apr. 3, 1924: 232.   AP201.Y8, v. 98

1132
Turkey denounces five centuries of calumny; text of Ismet Pasha's address at the Lausanne conference. Current history, v. 17, Feb. 1923: 749-757.
D410.C8, v. 17

1133
Turkey and the East. Atlantic monthly, v. 132, Oct. 1923: 546-555. AP2.A8, v. 132

1134
Turkey: foreign policy. European economic and political survey, v. 4, Oct. 15, 1928: 140-142.
HC10.E28, v. 4

1135
Turkey and her suitors. Economist, v. 133, Nov. 19, 1938: 361-362. HG11.E2, v. 133

1136
Turkey, a key state. Round table, v. 28, Dec. 1937: 110-124. AP4.R6, v. 28

1137
Turkey in the European balance. Economist, v. 136, July 15, 1939: 111-112. HG11.E2, v. 136

1138
Turkey in evolution. Near East and India, v. 33, Apr. 12, 1928: 452. D461.G8, v. 33

1139
Turkey in strategic spot while dictator lies ill. Scholastic, v. 33, Nov. 5, 1938: 14. AP2.S295, v. 33

1140
Turkey inaugurates economic reforms. *In* U. S. Bureau of Foreign and Domestic Commerce. Commerce reports, no. 31, Aug. 3, 1931: 262-264.
HC.R21, no. 31

1141
Turkey. İstatistik Umum Müdürlüğü. Compte-rendu du recensement agricole de 1927. Angora, 1928. 140 p. HD2036.A3

1142
Turkey. İstatistik Umum Müdürlüğü. Compte-rendu du recensement industriel de 1927. Angora, 1928. 140 p. HC401.A3

1143
Turkey and Lausanne. Near east, v. 22, Nov. 23, 1922: 668. D461.G8, v. 22

1144
Turkey. Matbuat Umum Müdürlüğü. Les actes d' atrocité et de la brutalité commises par les armées grècques en Anatolie. Ankara, Martbuat ve İstihbarat Matbaası, 1922, 214 p.

1145
Turkey. Matbuat Umum Müdürlüğü. La guerre de l'indépendance turque. İstanbul, Imp. d'état, 1937. 127 p. DR589.A46

1146
Turkey. Matbuat Umum Müdürlüğü. L'instruction publique en Turquie républicaine. Ankara, L' imprimerie d'état, 1936. 69 p. LA942.A45

1147
Turkey. Matbuat Umum Müdürlüğü. La Turquie contemporaine. Ankara, Imp. d'état, 1935. 304 p.
DR590.A5

1148
Turkey. Near East and India, v. 42, Nov. 2, 1933: 899-913. D461.G8, v. 42

1149
Turkey; old and very new. Sphere, v. 124, Feb. 21, 1931: 277-278. AP4.S73, v. 124

1150
Turkey on trial. Outlook, v. 145, Feb. 2, 1927: 135.
AP2.O8, v. 145

1151
Turkey and the powers. Quarterly review, v. 239, Jan. 1923: 161-182. AP4.Q2, v. 239

1152
Turkey: rampart in the Middle East. Army information digest, v. 7, May 1952: 34-48. U1.A827, v. 7

1153
Turkey: return to power. An Cosantoir, v. 15, Feb. 1955: 65-75. U1.C8, v. 15
Signed: D.N.B.

1154
Turkey, Russia and ourselves. New statesman, v. 26, Jan. 2, 1926: 348-349. AP4.N64, v. 26

1155
Turkey: the second five-year plan. Economist, v. 128, Sept. 24, 1937: 471-472. HG11.E2, v. 128

1156
Turkey. Treaties, etc., 1923-1938 (Atatürk) Traité d'
amitié entre la Turquie et la Bulgarie. Signé à Angora le 18 octobre 1925. Ankara, 1925.   JX847.A5

1157
Turkey. Türkofis. Commercial directory of Turkey.
Ankara, 1937. 492 p.   HF3713.A5

1158
Turkey. Türkofis. L'industrie minière de la Tur-
quie. Istanbul, Devlet Basımevi, 1935. 57 p.
TN93.A5

1159
Turkey. Unesco Türkiye Millî Komisyonu. Atatürk,
1881-1938. Ankara, Commission nationale turque
pour l'Unesco, 1963. 80 p.   DR592.K4787

1160
Turkey. Unesco Türkiye Millî Komisyonu. Atatürk,
1881-1938. Hommage de la Commission nationale
turque pour l'Unesco à l'occasion du vingt-cin-
quième anniversaire de sa mort, 10 novembre
1963. Ankara, 1963, 308 p.   DR592.K4A49

1161
Turkey and the West. Near east and India, v. 30,
Oct. 21, 1926: 445.   D461.G8, v. 30

1162
Turkey: working the new regime. Board of trade
journal and commercial gazette, v. 115, July 30,
1925: 118-121.   HF183.B8, v. 115

1163
Turkey's disciplined economic revolution. *In* Amer-
ican Academy of Political and Social Science.
Annals, v. 192, July 1937: 197-199.   HL.A4, v. 192

1164
Turkey's latest hero. Current opinion, v. 70, Mar.
1921: 331-333.   AP2.C95, v. 70

1165
Turkey's long furrow. Near east and India, v. 33,
Jan. 12, 1928: 35.   D461.G8, v. 33

1166
Turkey's "national pact." Current history, v. 17,
Nov. 1922: 280-281.   D410.C8, v. 17

1167
Turkish facts and fantasies. Foreign affairs, v. 3,
July 1925: 589-603.   D410.F6, v.
Signed: E.

1168
The Turkish government and religion. Missionary
review of the world, v. 47, Apr. 1924: 335-336.
BV2350.M7, v. 47

1169
Turkish in Latin characters. Near east and India,
v. 34, Aug. 30, 1928: 241.   D461.G8, v. 34

1170
A Turkish milestone. Near east and India, v. 32, Oct.
27, 1927: 516.   D461.G8, v. 32

1171
A Turkish presidential message of 400,000 words.
Literary digest, v. 95, Nov. 19, 1927: 16-17.
AP2.L58, v. 95

1172
The Turkish railway system. Geographical journal,
v. 95, Jan. 1940: 55-66.   G7.R91, v. 95

1173
The Turkish republic: aspects of domestic policy in
the domain of Mustapha Kemal. Asia, v. 24, Jan.
1924: 43-45.   HF3119.A5, v. 24

1174
The Turkish treaty—a symposium. Forum. v. 73,
Jan. 1925: 136-139.   AP2.F8, v. 73

1175
The Turkish victory. Nation, v. 115, Oct. 1922: 429.
AP2.N2, v. 115

1176
The Turkish victory at Lausanne. Current opinion,
v. 75, Sept. 1923: 277-278.   AP2.C95, v. 75

1177
Turkish women as pioneers. International review
of missions, v. 17, Oct. 1928: 645-654.
BV2351.I6, v. 17

1178
The Turks and the Patriarch. Outlook, v. 139, Apr.
29, 1925: 644-645.   AP2.O8, v. 139

1179
Turks and the treaty, with the reply of M. Venizelos.
Balkan review, v. 4, Aug. 1920: 69-77.
                                    D461.B3, v. 4

1180
Turlington, Edgar W. The American treaty of Lausanne. World peace foundation pamphlets, v. 7,
1924: 565-603.   JX1908.U5, v. 7

1181
Turlington, Edgar W. Peace with Turkey? Independent, v. 116, May 1, 1926: 514-516.   AP2.I53, v. 116

1182
Turlington, Edgar W. The settlement at Lausanne.
American journal of international law, v. 18, Oct.
1924: 696-706.   JX1.A6, v. 18

1183
Turlington, Edgar W. Treaty relations with Turkey.
Yale law journal, v. 35, Jan. 1926: 326-343.
                                    K29.A4, v. 35

1184
La Turquie à la Societé des Nations. L'Asie française, v. 32, juil.-août 1932: 225-228.
                                    JV1801.A85, v. 32

Signed: H. F.

1185
La Turquie en chiffres. Ankara, Imp. d'État, 1937.
108 p.   HC405.A4

1186
La Turquie en 1937. Journal des économistes, v. 108,
mars 1938: 249-255.   HB3.J8, v. 108

1187
Turquie; la fin du parti libéral. L'Asie française, v.
30, déc. 1930: 423.   JV1801.A85, v. 30

1188
Tveritinova, A. S. Fal'sifikatsiia istorii sredneve-
kovoĭ Turtsii v Kemalistskoĭ istoriografii. Vizanti-
iskii vremennki, v. 7, 1953: 9-31. DF501.V48, v. 7

1189
Tweedy, Owen. Turkey in step with twentieth century
civilization. Current history, v. 29, Nov. 1928:
247-251.   D410.C8, v. 29

1190
Tweedy, Owen. Turkey, romance and a diary. Atlantic monthly, v. 143, Mar. 1929: 390-400.
                                    AP2.A8, v. 143

1191
U.S. Dept. of State. Office of Public Affairs. The
problem of the Dardanelles, a summary of back-
ground information. Washington, Office of Public
Affairs, Dept. of State, 1946. 13 p.   DR701.D2U5

1192
U.S. Tariff Commission. Trade agreement between
the United States and the Republic of Turkey.
Washington, 1939. 125 p.   HF1732.T9A5

1193
U.S. Treaties, etc., 1929-1933 (Hoover) Establishment
and sojourn. Treaty between the United States of
America and the Turkish republic. Signed at An-
kara, October 28, 1931. Washington, U.S. Govt.
Print. Off., 1933. 3 p.   JX235.9A3 no. 859

1194
Ünal, Halit F. L'économie mixte en Turquie. Genève, Imp. Centrale, 1948. 176 p.   HC405.U34

1195
Uğurel, Refia. L'éducation de la femme en Turquie.,
Paris, Librairie philosophique J. Vrin, 1936. 150 p.

1196
Uhrenbacher, Werner J. Türkei; ein wirtschaftliches
handbuch. Berlin, E. Schmidt, 1957. 226 p.
                                    HC405.U35

1197
Uncle Sam mixing in the Turkish broil. Literary
digest, v. 75, Dec. 1923: 12-13.   AP2.L58, v. 75

1198
The United States and Turkey. Near east and India,
v. 31, Jan. 27, 1927: 75.   D461.G8, v. 31

1199
Usborne, C. V. Turkey's westernizing movement.
Great Britain and east, v. 48, May 13, 1937: 694-695.
                                    D461.G8, v. 48

1200
Vaidis, Toma A. Kemal Atatürk. Athēnai, Akropolis,
1936. 192 p.

1201
Vaka, D. Conversations with a Kemalist. Asia, v. 22,
Mar. 1922: 201-205.   HF3119.A5, v. 22

1202
Váli, Ferenc A. Bridge across the Bosporus; the for-
eign policy of Turkey. Baltimore, Johns Hopkins
Press, 1971. 410 p.   DR471.V3

1203
Váli, Ferenc A. The Turkish Straits and NATO. Stanford, Calif., Hoover Institution Press, 1972. 348 p.
          JX1393.S8V34

1204
Valyi, Felix. Turkey and the future of Islam. New
Orient, v. 2, July-Sept. 1925: 1-14.
          DS501.N6, v. 2

1205
Varsenko, A. Turt͡siia i vooruzhennye sily. Moskva,
Gos. Izd. Lit., 1928. 64 p.   JX231.A3 no. 133.4

1206
Vasilev, Ivan V. O turetskom neĭtralitete vo Vtoroĭ
Mirovoĭ voĭne. Moskva, Gos. izd-vo polit. litry,
1951. 118 p.   DR590.V3

1207
Vaucher, Robert. A Lausanne; les turcs devant les
alliés. L'Europe nouvelle, v. 5, 25 nov. 1922: 1480-
1481.   AP20.E88, v. 5

1208
Vdovichenko, Dmitrii I. Borba politichoskikh par-
tiĭ v Turt͡sii, 1944-1965 gg. Moskva, Nauka, 1967.
308 p.   JN9798.A1V4

1209
Vegh, Jenö. A tizéves Török köztarsasăg. Budapest,
1933. 80 p.

1210
Veinoglou, Al. Les origines de la République Turque.
Les Balkans, v. 4, août 1933: 400-435.
          DR1.B35, v. 4

1211
Velikov, Stefan. Kemalistkata revoliutsiia i bulgars-
kata obshtestvenost, 1918-1922. Sofiia, Izd-vo na
Bulgarskata akademiia na naukite, 1966. 129 p.
          DR73.T8V45

1212
Vellay, Charles. La perte de l'Ásie et ses conséquences. L'Europe nouvelle, v. 5, 30 sept. 1922: 1230-
1232.   AP20.E88, v. 5

1213
Vellay, Charles. La victoire turque. L'Europe nouvelle, v. 5, 16 sept. 1922: 1157-1161.
          AP20.E88, v. 5

1214
Veltman, Mikhail L. Revoliutsnonnaĭa Turt͡siia.
Moskva, Gosizdat, 1921. 127 p.

1215
Veninda. The significance of Turkish reform. World
dominion, v. 7, Apr. 1929: 160-164. BV2000.W6, v. 7

1216
Vere-Hodge, Edward R. Turkish foreign policy,
1918-1948. Ambilly-Annemasse, Imprimerie Franco. 1950. 215 p.   DR590.V4

1217
Vessaz, D. Ghazi on a tour. Living age, v. 327, Oct.
31, 1925: 230-231.   AP2.L65, v. 327

1218
Villari, Luigi. Da Mustafà Kemal a Kemal Atatürk.
Nuova antologia, v. 400, dic. 1, 1938: 326-334.
          AP37.N8, v. 400

1219
Visscher, Fernand de. La nouvelle convention des
Détroits. Revue de droit international et de légis-
lation comparée, n. s. v. 17, no. 4, 1936: 669-718.
          JX3.R35, v. 17

1220
Vissec, Lucien de. La Turquie et les minorités. Revue de Paris, v. 38, 1 avril 1931: 661-685.
          AP20.R27, v. 38

1221
Viton, Albert. The powers clash in Ankara. Common
sense, v. 8, Aug. 1939: 13-15.   JK1.C64, v. 8

1222
Vozhd Kemalizma o sebe, o partii. Biulleten pressy
srednego vostoka, no. 12, 1931: 44-46.
          DS1.B5, no. 12

1223
Vrooman, Helen. Turkey, a social laboratory. American scholar, v. 2, Mar. 1933: 243-244.
AP2.A4572, v. 2

1224
Vrooman, Lee. The meaning of the Turkish revolution. World tomorrow, v. 12, June 1929: 263-264.
HN51.W6, v. 12

1225
Vrooman, Lee. The place of missions in the new Turkey. International review of missions, v. 18, July 1929: 401-409.
BV2351.I6, v. 18

1226
Vrooman, Lee. Recent tendencies in Turkish education. Moslem world, v. 17, Oct. 1927: 370-374.
DS36.M7, v. 17

1227
Vrooman, Lee. Schools in Smyrna after ten years of the Turkish republic. School and society, v. 39, Jan. 20, 1934: 86-87.
L11.S36, v. 39

1228
Vrooman, Lee. A Turkish interpretation of world history. Moslem world, v. 23, Apr. 1933: 143-147.
DS36.M7, v. 23

1229
Walder, David. The Chanak affair. London, Hutchinson, 1969. 380 p.
DR589.W3

1230
Walsh, John R., *and* Andrew J. Mango. Turkey. *In* The encyclopedia Americana. New York, Americana Corp., 1972, v. 27. p. 248-273.
AE5.E333

1231
Walz, Jay. The Middle East. Chicago, Encyclopedia Britannica Press, 1965. 90 p.
DS62.W32

1232
The war after the war. Economist, v. 95, Sept. 9, 1922: 420-421.
HG11.E2, v. 95

1233
Warne, Osmund H. Your guide to Turkey. London, Redman, 1966. 231 p.
DR416.W3

1234
Warsamy, Georges D. La convention des Détroits;

Montreux 1936. Paris, A. Pedone, 1937. 158 p.
D462 1936 m

1235
Was Ismet bluffing? Independent, v. 110, Feb. 17, 1923: 111-112.
AP2.I53, v. 110

1236
Watt, D. C. The experience of opposition parties in Turkey. Quarterly review, v. 299, Jan. 1961: 56-63.
AP4.Q2, v. 299

1237
Waugh, *Sir* Telford. A far reaching Turkish plan. *In* Royal Central Asian Society. Journal, v. 20, Oct. 1933: 578-586.
DS1.R6, v. 20

1238
Waugh, *Sir* Telford. Nine years of republic in Turkey. *In* Royal Central Asian Society. Journal, v. 20, Jan. 1933: 52-69.
DS1.R6, v. 20

1239
Waugh, *Sir* Telford. Turkey; yesterday, today and tomorrow. London, Chapman & Hall, 1930. 305 p.
DR440.W3

1240
Webb, *Sir* Richard. The problem of the Straits. *In* Royal Central Asian Society. Journal, v. 18, July 1931: 307-334.
DS1.R6, v. 18

1241
Webster, Donald E. State control of social change in republican Turkey. American sociological review, v. 4, Apr. 1939: 247-256.
HM1.A75, v. 4

1242
Webster, Donald E. The Turkey of Atatürk; social process in the Turkish reformation. Philadelphia, The American Academy of Political and Social Science, 1939. 337 p.
DR589.W4

1243
Weigert, Oscar. New Turkish labor code. International labor review, v. 35, June 1937: 753-774.
HD4811.I65, v. 35

1244
Weiker, Walter F. The Free Party of 1930 in Turkey. Ph.D. dissertation, Dept. of Politics. Princeton University, Princeton, N.J. 1962.

1245
Weiker, Walter F. Turkey. *In* Ismael, Tareq Y. Governments and politics of the contemporary Middle East. Homewood, Ill., Dorsey Press, 1970. p. 125-149.
DS62.8.I83

1246
Weiker, Walter F. The Turkish revolution 1960-1961; aspects of military politics. Washington, Brookings Institution, 1963. 172 p.   DR590.W4

1247
Westermann, William L. Who are the Turks? Asia, v. 22, Dec. 1922: 985-989, 1013.   HF3119.A5, v. 22

1248
What Turkey won at Lausanne. Literary digest, v. 78, Aug. 4, 1923: 17.   AP2.L58, v. 78

1249
Wheeler, Everett P. American missionaries in Turkey. Current history, v. 17, Nov. 1922: 300-302.
D410.C8, v. 17

1250
Wheeler, Everett P. The power of the President to protect American citizens in Turkey and their work. Outlook, v. 132, Nov. 1, 1922: 370.
AP2.O8, v. 132

1251
White, W. W. Turkey enters world politics. Events, v. 6, Aug. 1939: 128-132.   D410.E845, v. 6

1252
White, W. W. Turkey keeps her balance. Events, v. 6, Dec. 1939: 453-456.   D410.E845, v. 6

1253
Why Angora expelled the Caliph; Turkish president plans divorce of state and church. Current opinion, v. 76, May 1924: 691-693.   AP2.C95, v. 76

1254
Why the democrats defeated the Turkish treaty. Literary digest, v. 92, Jan. 29, 1927: 10-11.   AP2.L58, v. 92

1255
Willett, Herbert L. Turkey has changed. Christian century, v. 48, Jan. 7, 1931: 14-16.   BR1.C45, v. 48

1256
Williams, Gwyn. Turkey: a traveller's guide and history. London, Faber, 1967. 318 p.   DR429.W5

1257
Williams, Kenneth. The emergence of Turkey. Fortnightly review, v. 147, Mar. 1937: 328-336.
AP4.F7, v. 147

1258
Williams, Kenneth. Is Turkey deserting Islam? Great Britain and east, v. 50, May 5, 1938: 485.
D461.G8, v. 50

1259
Williams, Kenneth. The key position of Turkey. Great Britain and east, v. 52, May 4, 1939: 495.
D461.G8, v. 52

1260
Williams, Kenneth. What is young Turkey thinking. Sphere, v. 135, Nov. 11, 1933: 218.   AP4.S73, v. 135

1261
Williams, Maynard O. Summer holidays on the Bosporus. National geographic magazine, v. 56, Oct. 1929: 487-508.   G1.N27, v. 56

1262
Williams, Maynard O. Turkey paves the path of progress. National geographic magazine, v. 100, Aug. 1951: 141-186.   G1.N27, v. 100

1263
Williams, Maynard O. Turkey, where earthquakes followed Timur's trail. National geographic magazine, v. 77, Mar. 1940: 395-406.   G1.N27, v. 77

1264
Wilson, Lucy L. Children in the new Turkey. American political science review, v. 62, Sept. 1, 1929: 560-563.   JA1.A6, v. 62

1265
Wilson, Lucy L. Education in the republic of Turkey. School and society, v. 28, Nov. 17, 1928: 601-610.
L11.S36, v. 28

1266
Wirsing, Giselher. Mustafa Kemal. *In his* Köpfe der Weltpolitik. München, Verlag Knorr und Hirth, 1934. p. 35-48.   D412.6.W5

1267

Wood, Margaret M. Latinizing the Turkish alphabet. American journal of sociology, v. 35, Sept. 1929: 194-203.   HM1.A7, v. 35

1268

Woodhouse, Henry. The Anglo-French conflict over Turkey. Current history, v. 16, Apr. 1922: 57-72.   D410.C8, v. 16

1269

Woods, H. Charles. The Anatolian war. Fortnightly review, v. 116, Sept. 1921: 492-500.   AP4.F7, v. 116

1270

Woods, H. Charles. The capitulations and Christian privileges in Turkey. Contemporary review, v. 122, Dec. 1922: 697-706.   AP4.C7, v. 122

1271

Woods, H. Charles. Ghazi Mustapha Kemal Pasha: his career, power and achievements. Fortnightly review, v. 128, Nov. 1927: 637-647.   AP4.F7, v. 128

1272

Woods, H. Charles. Lausanne and its accessories. Fortnightly review, v. 120, July 1923: 122-133.   AP4.F7, v. 120

1273

Woods, H. Charles. Lausanne and its antecedents. Fortnightly review, v. 119, Jan. 1923: 137-152.   AP4.F7, v. 119

1274

Woods, H. Charles. Lord Curzon and Lausanne. Fortnightly review, v. 119, Mar. 1923: 491-502.   AP4.F7, v. 119

1275

Woods, H. Charles. The new Turkey. Fortnightly review, v. 120, Sept. 1923: 363-371.   AP4.F7, v. 120

1276

Woods, H. Charles. Sèvres; before and after. Fortnightly review, v. 118, Oct. 1922: 545-560.   AP4.F7, v. 118

1277

Woods, H. Charles. The Straits; before and after. Fortnightly review, v. 119, Feb. 1923: 282-292.   AP4.F7, v. 119

1278

Woods, H. Charles. Turkey and Greece. Fortnightly review, v. 117, Feb. 1922: 332-340.   AP4.F7, v. 117

1279

Woods, H. Charles. Turkey under the nationalists. Contemporary review, v. 128, Nov. 1925: 584-591.   AP4.C7, v. 128

1280

Woods, H. Charles. Turkey yesterday and tomorrow. Quarterly review, v. 250, Apr. 1928: 368-384.   AP4.Q2, v. 250

1281

Woodsmall, Ruth F. Turkish women today. Independent woman, v. 13, Jan. 1934: 10-11.   HD6050.N3, v. 13

1282

Woolworth, William S., *Jr.* The moslem mind in Turkey today. Moslem world, v. 17, Apr. 1927: 139-146.   DS36.M7, v. 17

1283

Wortham, Hugh E. Mustapha Kemal of Turkey. Boston, Little, Brown, 1931. 251 p.   DR592.K4W6

1284

Wortham, Hugh E. Mustapha Kemal sets the styles. Atlantic monthly, v. 147, Mar. 1931: 356-366.   AP2.A8, v. 147

1285

Wright, Walter L. *Jr.* Truths about Turkey. Foreign affairs, v. 26, Jan. 1948: 349-359.   D410.F6, v. 26

1286

Wright, Walter L. *Jr.* Turkish crescent points East and West. American scholar, v. 7, July 1938: 259-267.   AP2.A4572, v. 7

1287

Wyatt, Stanley C. The economic and financial situation in Turkey: some observations with discussion. *In* Royal Central Asian Society. Journal, v. 21, Apr. 1934: 216-236.   DS1.R6, v. 21

1288

Wyatt, Stanley C. Turkey: the economic situation and the five-year plan. International affairs, v. 13, Nov. -Dec. 1934: 826-844.   JX1.I53, v. 13

1289
Yalçın, Aydın. Turkey: emerging democracy. Foreign affairs, v. 45, July 1967: 706-714.
D410.F6, v. 45

1290
Yale, William. The Near East; a modern history. Ann Arbor, University of Michigan Press, 1968. 485 p.
DS62.

1291
Yalman, Ahmet E. Turkey in my time. Norman, University of Oklahoma Press, 1956. 294 p.
DR590.

1292
Yate, A. C. The Near East. Asiatic review, v. 19, Jan. 1923: 18-23.
DS1.A7, v. 19

1293
Ybarra, T. R. Turkish delight: Atatürk. Collier's, v. 96, Dec. 21, 1935: 25, 64-66.
AP2.C65, v. 96

1294
Young, Sir George, bart. Constantinople. London, Methuen, New York, George H. Doran, 1926. 310 p.
DR728.Y6

1295
Zajaczkowska, Maria E. Kemal Pasza. Warszawa, Ksiażka i Wiedza, 1966. 305 p.
DR592.K4Z25

1296
Zapp, Manfred. Türkischer national Sozialismus. Preussische jahrbücher, v. 233, Aug. 1933: 105-112.
AP30.P8, v. 233

1297
Zara, Philipe de. Mustapha Kémal, dictateur. Paris, F. Sorlot, 1936. 370 p.
DR592.K4Z3

1298
Zavriev, D. S. Ekonomika sovremennoi Turt͡sii. Tbilisi, Zakgiz, 1934. 194 p.

1299
Zavriev, D. S. Knoveĭsheĭ istorii severovostochnykh vilaĭetov Turt͡sii. Tbilisi, Izd. Tbilissko go gos. universiteta, 1947. 367 p.
DR589.Z3

1300
Zavriev, D. S. Vostochnai͡a Anatolii͡a. Tiflis, Zakavk. torg. palata, 1936. 315 p.

1301
Ziemke, Kurt. Die neue Türkei; politische Entwicklung, 1914-1929. Stuttgart, Deutsche Verlagsanslalt, 1930. 549 p.
DR476.Z5

1302
Zingarelli, Italo. Il risveglio dell'Islam; la Turchia senza Corano; Russi e inglesi in Oriente. Milano, Fratelli Treves Editori, 1928. 261 p.
NN
ICU

1303
Ziya, Bedi. Grundlegung einer türkischen Erziehung aus türkischen Volkstum. Giessen, Druckerei J. Christ, 1937. 83 p.
LA942.Z5

1304
Les zones neutres des détroits et leurs variations. L'Asie française, v. 22, déc. 1922: 447-449.
JV1801.A85, v. 22

Signed: "M. F"

1305
Arrival of Ambassador Grew. Levant trade review, v. 15, Sept. 1927: 371-373.　　　　HF41.L4, v. 15

1306
Ataöv, Türkkaya. Turkish foreign policy: 1923-1938. *In* Milletlerarası münasebetler Türk yıllığı, 1961. Ankara, Institute of International Relations, 1963. p. 103-142.　　　　DR401.M55

1307
Bachman, Robert A. The American navy and the Turks. The Outlook, v. 132, Oct. 18, 1922: 288-289.　　　　AP2.08, v. 132

1308
Baker, Robert L. State planning in Turkey. Current history, v. 33, July 1933: 504-506.　　　　D410.C8, v. 33

1309
Barton, James L. Missionary problems in Turkey. International review of missions, v. 16, Oct. 1927: 481-494.　　　　BV2351.I6, v. 16

1310
Batu, Hâmit. La politique etrangère de la Turquie. *In* Milletlerarası münasebetler Türk yıllığı, 1964. Ankara, Institute of International Relations, 1966. p. 1-12.　　　　DR401.M55

1311
Bilsel, Cemil. The Turkish straits in the light of recent Turkish-Soviet Russian correspondence. American journal of international law, v. 41, Oct. 1947: 727-747.　　　　JX1.A6, v. 41

1312
Blaisdell, D. C. American investment in Turkey: a forecast. Levant trade review, v. 15, Dec. 1927: 521-529.　　　　HF41.LC, v. 15

1313
Edib, Halide (Adıvar). Dictatorship and reforms in Turkey. Yale review, v. 19, Sept. 1929: 27-44.　　　　AP2.Y2, v. 19

1314
Edib, Halide (Adıvar). Home from the war. Asia, v. 28, Oct. 1928: 782-789, 843-849.　　　　HF3119.A5, v. 28

1315
Edib, Halide (Adıvar). My share in the Turkish ordeal. Asia, v. 28, June 1928: 437-443, 509-515.　　　　HF3119.A5, v. 28

1316
Edib, Halide (Adıvar). Poor Turks, poor Greeks, poor world. Asia, v. 28, Aug. 1928: 638-645, 654-661.　　　　HF3119.A5, v. 28

1317
Edib, Halide (Adıvar). A woman soldier at the front. Asia, v. 28, Sept. 1928: 700-707, 747-752.　　　　HF3119.A5, v. 28

1318
Esmer, Ahmed Ş. The straits: crux of world politics. Foreign affairs, v. 25, Jan. 1947: 290-302.　　　　D410.F6, v. 25

1319
Gates, Caleb F. The departure of Admiral Bristol. Levant trade review, v. 15, May 1927: 183-186.　　　　HF41.L4, v. 15

1320
Gugliemotti, Umberto. Ataturk. *In his* I dittatori. Roma, C.E.N., 1972. p. 841-941.　　　　D412.G84, v. 2

1321
Heck, Lewis. Sidelights on past relations between the

United States and Turkey. American foreign service journal, v. 17, Feb. 1940: 61-63, 110-114.
JX1.A53, v. 17

1322
Hotham, David. The Turks. London, John Murray, 1972. 220 p.   DR417.H67

1323
Howard, Harry N. The United States and the problem of the Turkish straits, a reference article. Middle East journal, v. 1, Jan. 1947: 59-72. DS1.M5, v. 1

1324
Kazdal, Mustafa N. Trade relations between the United States and Turkey, 1919-1944. Ph.D. thesis, Indiana University, Ind. 1946.

1325
Kiosseoglou, Th. P. L'échange forcé des minorités d'après le traité de Lausanne. These de droit, Nancy, 1926. 218 p.

1326
Köymen, Oya B. Anglo-Turkish relations, 1919-22. *In* Milletlerarası münasebetler Türk yıllığı, 1967. Ankara, Institute of International Relations, 1970. p. 14-28.   DR401.M55

1327
Lybyer, Albert H. Turkey's adoption of the Roman alphabet. Current history, v. 28, Aug. 1928: 880-881.
D410.C8, v. 28

1328
Morrison, Charles C. Turkey's dictator. Christian century, v. 52, June 26, 1935: 847-849.
BR1.C45, v. 52

1329
Özbuden, Ergun. The role of the military in recent Turkish politics. Cambridge, Center for International Affairs, Harvard University, 1966. 54 p.
JN9720.C503

1330
Pipinelis, Panayotis. The Greko-Turkish feud revived. Foreign affairs, v. 37, Jan. 1959: 306-316.
D410.F6, v. 37

1331
Psomiades, Harry J. The ecumenical patriarchate under the Turkish Republic: the first ten years. New York, Greek Archdiocese of North and South America, 1964. 80 p.   BX410.P74

1332
Sachar, Howard M. The United States and Turkey, 1914-1927: the origins of Near Eastern policy. Ph.D. thesis, Harvard University, Cambridge, Mass.,   1953.

1333
Toynbee, Arnold J. *ed.,* Abolition of Ottoman Caliphate. *In* Survey of international affairs, 1925. London, Oxford University Press, 1927. p. 25-91.
D442.S8

1334
Toynbee, Arnold J. *ed.,* The Kurdish revolt in Turkey, February to April 1925. *In* Survey of international affairs, 1925. London, Oxford University Press, 1927. p. 507-511.   D442.S8

1335
Toynbee, Arnold J. *ed.* Relations between Soviet Russia, the Trancaucasian republics, and Turkey from the armistice of Mudros (30th Oct. 1918) to the signature of the treaty of Lausanne (24th July, 1923). *In* Survey of international affairs, 1920-1923. New York, Oxford University Press, 1925. p. 361-376.   D442.S8

1336
Treaty relations between the Turkish Republic and the United States. Levant trade review, v. 16, April 1928: 138.   HF41.L4, v. 16

1337
Turco-American relations. Current history, v. 38, June 1933: 379.   D410.C8, v. 38

1338
Van Norman, Louis E. Ten years of the new Turkey— an economic retrospect. The open court, v. 46, May 1932: 320-330.   AP2.O495, v. 46

Periodical Sources Utilized

Title	Location	Year Established	LC Call Number
Action nationale	Paris, France	1917	AP20.A3
Advocate of peace (World affairs)	Washington, D.C.	1837	JX1901.W7
American academy of political and social science. Annals	Philadelphia, Pa.	1890	H1.A4
American anthropologist	Menasha, Wis.	1888	GN1.A5
American association of petroleum geologists. Bulletin	Tulsa, Okla.	1917	TN860.A3
American foreign service journal	Washington, D.C.	1924	JX1.A53
American historical review	New York, N.Y.	1895	E171.A57
American journal of international law	Washington, D.C.	1907	JX1.A6
American political science review	Menasha, Wis.	1906	JA1.A6
American review	Bloomington, Ill.	1923	AP2.A43
American review of reviews (Review of reviews)	New York, N.Y.	1889	AP2.R4
American scholar	Concord, N. H.	1932	AP2.A4572
American sociological review	Menasha, Wis.	1936	HM1.A75
An Cosantoir	Dublin, Ireland	1940	U1.C8
Annaly	Leningrad, USSR	1922	D1.A5
Army information digest	Washington, D. C.	1946	U1.A827
Army quarterly	London, England	1920	U1.A85
Asia	New York, N. Y.	1898	HF3119.A5
Asiatic review	London, England	1886	DS1.A7

Title	Location	Year Established	LC Call Number
L'Asie française	Paris, France	1901	JV1801.A85
Atlantic monthly	Boston, Mass.	1857	AP2.A8
Aussenpolitik	Stuttgart, Germany	1950	D839.A885
Balkan review (Eastern Europe)	London, England	1919	D461.E3
Balkan studies	Thessaloniki, Greece	1960	DR1.B32
Les Balkans	Athens, Greece	1931	DR1.B35
Bankers', insurance managers' and agents' magazine	London, England	1844	HG1503.B2
Berliner monatshefte	Berlin, Germany	1923	D511.A1B4
Biulleten pressy srednego vostoka	Tashkent, USSR	1928	DS1.B5
Board of trade journal and commercial gazette	London, England	1886	HF183.B8
Bol'shevik (Kommunist)	Moscow, USSR	1924	HX8.K56
Boston city club bulletin	Boston, Mass.	1911	HS2725.B7C615
Builder	London, England	1842	NA1.B5
Bulletin of international news	London, England	1925	D410.B8
Business history review	Boston, Mass.	1926	HF500.B8262
Canada. Dept. of Trade and Commerce. Commercial intelligence journal	Ottawa, Canada	1909	HF129.A27
Century	New Delhi, India	1963	AP2.C4
Christian century	Chicago, Ill.	1884	BR1.C45
Collier's	Springfield, Ohio	1888	AP2.C65
Common sense	Chicago, Ill.	1947	JX1901.C68
Commonweal	New York, N. Y.	1924	AP2.C6897
Contemporary review	London, England	1866	AP4.C7
Correspondant	Paris, France	1868	AP20.C8
Current affairs	Ottawa, Canada	1951	D839.C863
Current history	New York, N. Y.	1914	D410.C8
Current opinion	New York, N. Y.	1888	AP2.O95
Dalhousie review	Halifax, Canada	1921	AP5.D3
Economic geography	Worcester, Mass.	1925	HF1021.E4
Economist	London, England	1830	HG11.E2

Title	*Location*	*Year Established*	*LC Call Number*
Edinburgh review	Edinburgh, Scotland	1802	AP4.E3
Èlet ès tudomány kalendariuma	Budapest, Hungary	1958	Q9.E45
Empire review	Binghamton, N. Y.	1958	DA10.C5
English review	London, England	1844	AP4.E523
Esercito e nazione (Nazione militare)	Rome, Italy	1925	U4.N38
Études	Paris, France	1897	AP20.E8
Europäische Revue	Leipzig, Germany	1925	AP30.E8
L'Europe nouvelle	Paris, France	1918	AP20.E88
European economic and political survey	Paris, France	1925	HC10.E8
Events	New York, N. Y.	1937	D410.E845
Foreign affairs	New York, N. Y.	1922	D410.F6
Foreign policy reports	New York, N. Y.	1925	D410.F65
Fortnightly review	London, England	1865	AP4.F7
Forum	Philadelphia, Pa.	1886	AP2.F8
Free Europe	London, England	1939	D731.F7
Geografiska annaler	Stockholm, Sweden	1919	G25.G4
Geographical magazine	London, England	1935	G1.G343
Geographical review	New York, N. Y.	1916	G1.G35
Geographische Zeitschrift	Wiesbaden, Germany	1895	G1.G37
Geographischer Anzeiger	Gotha, Germany	1900	G1.G39
Gerarchia	Milano, Italy	1920	D410.G43
La grande revue	Paris, France	1903	AP20.G7
Great Britain and east (Near east; Near east and India)	London, England	1908	D461.G8
Haagsch maandblad	Gravenhage, Netherlands	1924	AP15.H3
L'illustration	Paris, France	1843	AP20.I3
The Independent	New York, N. Y.	1848	AP2.I53
Independent woman (National business woman)	Washington, D. C.	1919	HD6050.N3
International affairs	London, England	1922	JX1.I53
International labor review	Geneva, Switzerland	1921	HD4811.I65
International review of missions	Edinburgh, Scotland	1912	BV2351.I6

Title	Location	Year Established	LC Call Number
Islamic review	Woking, England	1921	BP1.I7
Istoricheski pregled	Sofia, Bulgaria	1945	DR51.B883
Jewish frontier	New York, N. Y.	1933	DS149.A324
Jorden runt	Stockholm, Sweden	1929	G149.J54
Journal des économistes	Paris, France	1841	HB3.J8
Journal of American history	Abilene, Kan.	1914	E171.J87
Journal of applied sociology	Los Angeles, Calif.	1921	HM1.S75
Journal of geography	Chicago, Ill.	1902	G1.J87
Journal of politics	Gainesville, Fla.	1939	JA1.J6
Journal of religion	Chicago, Ill.	1921	BR1.J65
Kommunist (Bolshevik)	Moscow, USSR	1924	HX8.K56
Krasnayi internatsional profsoiuzov	Moscow, USSR	1921	HD6475.A2R34
Krasnaia nov'	Moscow, USSR	1921	AP50.K73
Kyklos	Bern, Switzerland	1947	H1.A15
Levant trade review	Istanbul, Turkey	1911	HF41.L4
Life	Chicago, Ill.	1936	AP2.L547
Life and letters today	London, England	1928	AP4.L416
Listener	London, England	1930	AP4.L4165
Literary digest	New York, N. Y.	1890	AP2.L58
Living age	New York, N. Y.	1844	AP2.L65
London quarterly review	London, England	1853	AP4.L54
Mentor	New York, N.Y.	1913	AP2.M417
Mercure de France	Paris, France	1890	AP20.M5
Mezhdunarodnaiâ Zhisn'	Moscow, USSR	1922	D410.M4
Middle East journal	Washington, D.C.	1947	DS1.M5
Military review	Fort Leavenworth, Kan.	1922	Z6723.U35
Mirovoe khoziaĭstvo i mirovaia politika	Moscow, USSR	1926	HC10.K536
Missionary review of the world	New York, N. Y.	1878	BV2350.M7
Le monde slave	Paris, France	1917	D461.M7
Moslem world	Hartford, Conn.	1911	DS36.M7
Narodnyi uchitel	Moscow, USSR	1924	Unclass. Cyr. N-9

Title	Location	Year Established	LC Call Number
Nation	New York, N. Y.	1865	AP2.N2
National geographic magazine	Washington, D. C.	1888	G1.N27
Near east (Near east and India; Gt. Britain and East)	London, England	1885	D461.G8
Near east and India (Near east; Gt. Brit. and east)	London, England	1885	D61.G8
New Armenia	New York, N. Y.	1904	DS161.N47
New Europe	London, England	1916	D410.N4
New leader	New York, N. Y.	1927	HX1.N37
New orient	New York, N. Y.	1923	DS501.N6
New republic	New York, N. Y.	1914	AP2.N624
New statesman	London, England	1913	AP4.N64
Newsweek	New York, N. Y.	1933	AP2.N6772
Nineteenth century and after	London, England	1877	AP4.N7
North American review	Mount Vernon, Iowa	1815	AP2.N7
Novyi vostok	Moscow, USSR	1922	YUDIN JN18.N9
Nuova antologia	Rome, Italy	1866	AP37.N8
Open court	Chicago, Ill.	1887	AP2.0495
L'opinion	Paris, France	1908	AP20.06
Orient	Paris, France	1957	DS1.044
Orient et occident	Paris, France	1921	DS1.045
Oriente moderno	Rome, Italy	1921	D461.07
Outlook	New York, N. Y.	1870	AP2.08
Petermanns geographishce Mitteilungen	Gotha, Germany	1855	G1.P43
Political quarterly	London, England	1930	JA8.P72
Political science quarterly	New York, N. Y.	1886	H1.P8
Politique étrangère	Paris, France	1935	JX3.P6
Preussische jahrbücher	Berlin, Germany	1858	AP30.P8
Quarterly review	London, England	1809	AP4.Q2
Rassegna di cultura militare	Rome, Italy	1938	U4.R25

Title	Location	Year Established	LC Call Number
Recreation	New York, N. Y.	1907	GV421.R5
Reporter	New York, N. Y.	1949	D839.R385
Review of politics	Notre Dame, Ind.	1939	JA1.R4
Revoliutsionnyĭ vostok	Moscow, USSR	1927	DS1.N353
Revue de droit international et de législation comparée	Brussels, Belgium	1869	JX3.R35
Revue de Genève (Bibliothèque Universelle et Revue de Genève)	Geneva, Switzerland	1920	AP24.B44
Revue de Paris	Paris. France	1894	AP20.R27
Revue des deux mondes	Paris, France	1881	AP20.R3
Revue des sciences politiques	Paris, France	1886	H3.R35
Revue économique internationale	Brussels, Belgium	1904	HB3.R5
Revue générale de droit international public	Paris, France	1894	JX3.R56
Revue hebdomadaire	Paris, France	1902	AP20.R55
Revue mondiale	Paris, France	1890	AP20.R25
Revue politique et parlementaire	Paris, France	1894	H3.R4
Rivista Italiana di scienze economiche	Bologna, Italy	1929	HB7.R5
Rivista militare Italiana	Rome, Italy	1901	U4.R57
Round table	London, England	1910	AP4.P6
Royal Central Asian Soceity. Journal	London, England	1914	DS1.R6
Royal Geographical Society. Journal	London, England	1918	G7.R91
Russia (1917-R.S.F.S.R.). Narodnoyi komissariat po inostrannym delam. Biŭlleten.	Moscow, USSR	1922	D411.R92
Saturday evening post	Philadelphia, Pa.	1821	AP2.S2
Saturday review	London, England	1855	AP4.S3
Scholastic	Pittsburgh, Pa.	1920	AP2.S295
School and society	New York, N.Y.	1915	L11.S36
Scribner's	New York, N. Y.	1887	AP2.S4
Social forces	Chapel Hill, N. C.	1922	HN51.S5

Title	Location	Year Established	LC Call Number
Social science	Winfield, Kan.	1925	H1.S55
Societa Geografica Italiana. Bolletino	Rome, Italy	1868	G17.S67
Sociology and social research	Los Angeles, Calif.	1921	HM1.S75
South Atlantic quarterly	Durham, N. C.	1902	AP2.S75
Soviet Russia	New York, N.Y.	1920	DK266.A287
Spectator	London, England	1828	AP4.S3
Sphere	London, England	1900	AP4.S73
Svensk geografish arsbok	Lund, Sweden	1925	G25.S8
Svensk tidskrift	Uppsala, Sweden	1911	AP48.S76
Swiss review of world affairs	Zürich, Switzerland	1951	D839.S9
Tiden	Stockholm, Sweden	1909	HX8.T5
Torgovlia SSSR s vostokom	Moscow, USSR	1923	HC331.T58
Transcaucasia (1922- S.F.S.R.). Vysshiĭ ékonomichesskiĭ sovet. Ekonomicheskiĭ vestnik zakavkaz'ia	Tbilisi, USSR	1924	HC337.T7A4
Travel	New York, N. Y.	1901	G149.T73
Turán	Budapest, Hungary	1918	DS1.T8
U. S. Bureau of Foreign and Domestic Commerce. Commerce reports	Washington, D. C.	1926	HC1.R21
United States Naval Institute proceedings	Annapolis, Md.	1874	V1.U8
University of Toronto quarterly	Toronto, Canada	1895	LH3.T6Q2
Vie del mondo	Milano, Italy	1932	G1.V53
Vizantiškiĭ vremennik	Moscow, USSR	1947	DF501.V48
Vysshaia shkola	Moscow, USSR	1936	LB2300.W6
World affairs interpreter	Los Angeles, Calif.	1930	AP2.W74825
World dominion	New York, N. Y.	1923	BV2000.W6
World peace foundation pamphlets	Boston, Mass.	1910	JX1908.U5
World politics	New Haven, Conn.	1948	D839.W57
World today	London, England	1902	AP4.W85

Title	Location	Year Established	LC Call Number
World tomorrow	New York, N. Y.	1918	HN51.W6
World unity	New York, N. Y.	1927	AP2.W755
World's work	New York, N. Y.	1900	AP2.W8
Yale law journal	New Haven, Conn.	1891	K29.A4
Yale review	New Haven, Conn.	1892	AP2.Y2
Youth's companion	Boston, Mass.	1827	AP201.Y8
Za partiiu	Tashkent, USSR	1927	JN6598.K4Z2
Zeitschrift für politik	Berlin, Germany	1907	JA14.Z4
Zivot i rad	Belgrade, Yugoslavia	1928	AP56.Z5

XIIV
15"